THE SPIRIT OF THE HUCKLEBERRY

The Spirit of the Huckleberry

SENSUOUSNESS IN HENRY THOREAU

Victor Carl Friesen

 The University of Alberta Press

First published by
The University of Alberta Press
Athabasca Hall
Edmonton, Alberta
Canada T6G 2E8

Copyright © The University of Alberta Press 1984

ISBN 0–88864–043–9

Canadian Cataloguing in Publication Data

Friesen, Victor Carl.
  The spirit of the huckleberry

  ISBN 0–88864–043–9

  1. Thoreau, Henry David, 1817–1862 —
Criticism and interpretation.   2. Senses
and sensation in literature.   I. Title.
PS3054.F75 1984   818'.309   C83–091493–5

Typesetting by Solaris Press, Inc., Rochester, Michigan

Printed by D.W. Friesen & Sons Ltd., Altona, Manitoba, Canada

To my parents, Anna and Abram Friesen, who in their life together practiced Thoreau's simple rural economy through necessity and enjoyed doing so

Contents

Abbreviations

The works of Henry David Thoreau have been cited in the text with abbreviations followed by the appropriate page number. Works frequently cited have been identified by the following abbreviations. (While some volumes of the new Princeton edition of Thoreau's works have already been published, it was felt that references to Thoreau here should be to a single source where possible in order to facilitate simple, ready accessibility.)

I   *The Writings of Henry David Thoreau*, 20 vols., Walden edn. (Boston: Houghton Mifflin, 1906), Vol. I, *A Week on the Concord and Merrimack Rivers*.

II   *The Writings of Henry David Thoreau*, 20 vols., Walden edn. (Boston: Houghton Mifflin, 1906), Vol. II, *Walden.*

III   *The Writings of Henry David Thoreau*, 20 vols., Walden edn. (Boston: Houghton Mifflin, 1906), Vol. III, *The Maine Woods.*

IV   *The Writings of Henry David Thoreau*, 20 vols., Walden edn. (Boston: Houghton Mifflin, 1906), Vol. IV, *Cape Cod and Miscellanies.*

V   *The Writings of Henry David Thoreau*, 20 vols., Walden edn. (Boston: Houghton Mifflin, 1906), Vol. V, *Excursions and Poems.*

VI   *The Writings of Henry David Thoreau*, 20 vols., Walden edn. (Boston: Houghton Mifflin, 1906), Vol. VI, *Familiar Letters.*

Preface

When Henry David Thoreau writes in his second book, *Walden*, 1854, that we "can never have enough of nature" (II, 35),[1] he is speaking, at least in part, of his own continuing sensuous approach to the outdoor world. In an early volume of his *Journal* he writes, "Employ your senses" (VIII, 251), and in the last volume he continues in this vein: "expressions of our delight which any natural object draws from us are something complete and final in themselves" (XX, 117). In his first book, *A Week on the Concord and Merrimack Rivers*, 1849, he speaks of wishing to live a "*purely* sensuous life" (I, 408). The emphasis on "purely" seems to suggest that his life be wholly sensuous, not necessarily excluding the rational life but plainly giving it a sensuous basis. "Purely" also seems to suggest "purity," so that a "purely sensuous life" would be one where the senses are undefiled by dissipation, a life where crystalline senses are extensively used in a wholesome appreciation of nature. A third suggested meaning could point to a life where one has a kind of supersensory perception, capable of hearing "celestial" sounds and capable of learning "that there is a nature behind the ordinary" (I, 409). Thoreau's sensitivity to puns would suggest that he has in mind all three meanings; the succeeding chapters of this book will show that he has.

Since the term "sensuous" has been much bandied about in current popular literature, it may be useful at this point to make a sharp distinction between "sensuousness" and another word with which it is often confused—"sensuality." Properly speaking, "sensuousness" is an amoral term. It refers simply to one's ability to perceive the world around him with his senses, an ability depending upon the acuity of the senses and upon their wide use.[2] "Sensuality," however, has moral — in this case, immoral — connotations. It is an indulgence of one's grosser appetites, something avoided by the high-minded Thoreau.

Most of Thoreau's closest friends made some mention of his sensuous character, of both the keenness of his senses and the varied use he put them to. Ralph Waldo Emerson referred to this trait in the funeral oration he delivered for Thoreau in 1862, although on the whole he was trying to praise the stoical nature of his friend. Thoreau "saw as with microscope, heard as with ear-trumpet" — is Emerson's emphatic note.[3] In a short tribute entitled "Thoreau" in *Concord Days*, 1872, A. Bronson Alcott says that Thoreau's senses seemed double; that he had "an instinct for seeing and judging, as by some other, or seventh sense."[4]

Emerson and Alcott perhaps tended to overemphasize the acuity of the younger man's senses; but a third acquaintance corroborates their view. William Ellery Channing was Thoreau's most frequent walking companion and therefore well able to say something about him, which he did in *Thoreau: The Poet-Naturalist*, 1873, the first full-length biography. In "Philosophy," the chapter which purports to give Thoreau's outlook, the author starts with a four-paragraph quotation from Thoreau's manuscript journals; and this is a typical passage: "When I see the sulphur lichens on the rails . . . , I feel like studying them again as a relisher or tonic, to make life go down and digest well, as we use pepper and vinegar and salads. They are a sort of wintergreens, which we gather and assimilate with our eyes."[5] Channing concludes that in such quotations Thoreau's life may be sought. Surely he wishes to depict Thoreau as a sensuous man.

When acquaintances were no longer living to report on Thoreau at firsthand, literary critics came to refer to his sensuousness in varying manner by basing their opinions on an analysis of his writings. (Although Thoreau published only two books in his lifetime, several collections of his writings were issued before the first full edition came out in 1906.) But only four or five of the critics have dealt with sensuousness at any length, and even then their remarks on this subject are often incidental. Thus Norman Foerster's principal concern is Thoreau's humanness (*Nature in American Literature*, 1923); F. O. Matthiessen's is the writings as works of art (*American Renaissance*, 1941); and Reginald L. Cook's is correspondence with nature (*Passage to Walden*, 1949).

More recently, Joel Porte brought out a book, *Emerson and Thoreau*, 1966, in which he points out the difference between the two and argues that Thoreau's position was diametrically opposite to that of Emerson and his notion of correspondence with nature. Thoreau, according to Porte, was really a Lockean, that is, someone who believed that all we know comes by way of the physical senses. Since his senses, like anyone else's, grew dull or decayed with age, Porte believes that not only did his art too become dull (Porte forgets that Thoreau still had a memory of former sensations and could relive them in his mind and record them) but also that such a "decay" in life and art was, for the Concord writer, a painful realization: in the face of death he lost his sensuous appetite for life and was actually undergoing a tragic struggle against it. (Later chapters here will come to a different conclusion.)

One further book can be included in this discussion, although it again deals with Thoreau's sensuousness in only a peripheral way. As its title suggests, James McIntosh's *Thoreau as Romantic Naturalist: His Shifting Stance toward Nature*, 1974, is really about the *changing* elements in Thoreau's relation to nature. But in delineating these elements, it does see his sensuousness as a kind of stable counterpoint. (The present book, like McIntosh's, also speaks of Thoreau's repeatedly trying to achieve a balance between opposite poles — involvement and observation *or* instinct and intellect — and always finding it an ungraspable phantom of life; the focus, however, is away from these things to the *constant* element — sensuousness. In this regard it is a kind of complement to McIntosh's work.)

Such, up to this time, have been the principal considerations voiced by various commentators on Thoreau's sensuousness. Some degree of this trait is the stock-in-trade of most writers, and a full awareness of its significance in him should have become a commonplace. Yet the end result of more than a century of criticism — as pointed out by Walter Harding, the distinguished Thoreau scholar — has generally been to reinforce Thoreau's image as a stoic and an ascetic. The impression left by Emerson's eulogy is that he was a man of renunciations. The impression left by modern critics, since they on the whole emphasize his Transcendentalism, is that he was one who "abjured the physical world and dwelt in the world of ideas."[6] They may recognize his sensuousness but tend to give it scant treatment. And those few critics, we have seen, who do make a case for his sensuousness have largely overlooked its pervasiveness—the implications it has for the whole spectrum of his life and thought.

My work, then, is a corrective—its purpose to show that sensuousness accounts for the essential Thoreau. It is mainly exposition and planned to be thorough without being exhaustive. The first chapters show how overwhelming this trait is in Thoreau's life—how he wishes to be attuned to each sight, sound, flavor, taste, and touch of nature individually. Doing so has implications for his notions about health and wildness because the extent to which his senses are stimulated is a measure of his health and because wildness is a condition dependent on sound physical senses. These chapters are largely descriptive of sensuousness in itself.

The succeeding chapters show the implications of sensuousness in other areas pertaining to Thoreau—in the areas of economics, writing style, science, and general philosophic outlook about man's relationship to nature. His stance in trying to be part of both the wild and the civilized worlds by alternating between them has its parallel in economic matters when he wants to live simply and extravagantly and so achieve the best of both worlds—and in literary matters where simple and extravagant styles complement each other to leave sensuous impressions. His stance, however, does not obtain for him the objectivity that a scientist needs. Instead, he gathers information about nature casually as he saunters outdoors. This activity is for him a spiritual experience, a time to have mystic insight and see the underlying unity of all of nature. With this kind of progression I hope to bring the sprawling subject of his approach to nature within reasonable compass.

Of course, there are other Thoreaus than the one portrayed here. McIntosh makes a similar statement about his own treatment of this writer, as do various critics. Perhaps what Geoffrey H. Hartman says in his preface to a study of Wordsworth's poetry states the case for all of us: "I do not consider my approach exclusive but sustaining a thesis required a certain purity in the matter of exposition."[7]

Mention of another writer, Wordsworth, brings up a further consideration. My approach is in keeping with the spirit of American

Transcendentalism—to waive intermediaries and go to the principal subject itself. In an expository treatment such as mine, I believe that the best way to study Thoreau is to go to his writing (the whole corpus) and see what he says.[8] Thus I am not trying to see him in light of a different author, of a literary period, or, even more removed, of somebody else's criticism, but rather trying to see him for himself. I know, however, that no writer exists in isolation, and I have considered influences on Thoreau *as called for*. I refer, as need arises, to Plato's pre-existent state, Gilpin's theory of the Picturesque, Ruskin's economics, and Suzuki's Zen Buddhism. Really, these sorts of things tend to be the stuff of undergraduate English courses, and it is probably my university career which prompts me to deal in this fashion at all, but I have tried to keep such references to a minimum. Again, I refer to Homer and Chaucer; Donne and Herbert; Bunyan and Quarles; Emerson and Whitman, among others, but I make no extended comparisons.

Wordsworth is somewhat another matter. Thoreau refers to him several times and quotes from him: some discussion of Thoreau and Wordsworth is called for (not however in a context of Romanticism— that area has been dealt with by McIntosh—but in the context of sensuousness). It is true that there are some interesting parallels between Romantic writers and Thoreau. A few critics have gone so far as to believe that he was thoroughly permeated by ideas of the late eighteenth century. But, as one would expect about any writer having the typical eclectic reading tastes of a New England Transcendentalist, there are such parallels to be found also between his writings and classical, oriental, Puritan, and metaphysical writing. Indeed, Foerster and Matthiessen would say that Thoreau's principal intellectual heritage stems from seventeenth-century writers. What I have tried to do is to give a fair sampling of contextual aspects (including those not narrowly Romantic), enough contextual aspects pertaining to my subject to abet my discussion of sensuousness without detracting from it. It should be apparent that I am rather wary of trying to see such a down-to-earth Yankee as Thoreau in terms of a superimposed framework. Critics, using this technique, have been able to "prove" that he is "a stoic or an epicurean, a pacifist or a militarist, a pessimist or an optimist, and individualist or a communist."[9] The truth is that Thoreau is his own man—and, I repeat, should be seen for himself.

My own introduction to Thoreau was not through university classes (where all too often, since chronologically he appears in texts after his fellow townsman Emerson, he is pictured as but a younger, and cantankerous, sage of Concord). I first read his work while living in my own isolated hut, the fourteen-by-twenty-foot teacherage of a one-roomed rural school near historic Fort Carlton, which was famous during the fur-trading days of the Canadian Northwest. Here it was that by the light of a coal-oil lamp I pored over the pages of *Walden*, while a great horned owl hooted from the roof top and where next morning I would awake to find deer tracks encircling my snug harbor in the woods.

Not only my surroundings but my interest in and knowledge of natural history gave me an insight into that major element in Thoreau which is not strictly literary—his naturalist's bent. He has been variously called the poet-naturalist, the philosopher-naturalist, and the social critic-naturalist: *naturalist* is the common denominator. Yet *literary* critics have continually slighted or misinterpreted this aspect of Thoreau. I hope that my treatment, although it must deal specifically with sensuousness, corrects this failing—the chapter on sensuousness and science is the longest in the book. And if this same background makes my treatment in that chapter, and others, highly appreciative, even a kind of celebration—well, I offer no excuse for its being so.

Comment should also be made on the writing style in this book. E. B. White, that master essayist and himself a commentator on Thoreau, has written: "There isn't any thought or idea which can't be expressed in a fairly simple declarative sentence, or in a series of fairly simple declarative sentences."[10] Taking this as my maxim, I have tried to avoid that convoluted style which so easily can creep into academic writing. Finally the reader should note that the present tense is deliberately used throughout in discussing Henry Thoreau. This approach is taken because the work is not properly about some overall development: the focus, as I have said, is on a *constant* in his life—sensuousness. (Walter Harding in his definitive biography, *The Days of Henry Thoreau*, 1966, observes that "at the very moment [Thoreau] was beginning to feel old, he was recording in his journal a sensuousness that any youth would envy."[11]) Still, individual chapters do show changes in those aspects of his thought which have relation to his

sensuousness — his economic views before and after his Walden experiment in Chapter 4, his increasing scientific bent in Chapter 6, and his
loss of mystic experiences with age in Chapter 7. However, it is mainly
the intention to present Thoreau as all of a piece, simultaneously, as it
were. Thus keeping to the present tense is in fact my metaphor to describe a man who continues to speak to us in our day (although what
he says to each decade may vary) and who is more widely known now
than ever. Not only that, but he is a man who also chooses in his own
life to live fully in the rich present moment of each day, as the next
chapter makes clear. His sensuousness, variously manifested, is an
ongoing feature of his adult life. Again: it marks the essential
Thoreau, and we have had time enough to arrive at this kind of
general assessment.

Acknowledgments

This book grew out of my studies at two separate graduate schools.
Therefore I am indebted to Dr. Morton L. Ross, of the University of
Alberta, Edmonton, who supervised my doctoral dissertation on
Thoreau and his sensuousness; and to Dr. Edward J. Rose, then head
of that university's English Department, who initially guided my proj-
ect. Both men gave most generously of their time and scholarship during
the course of my work. For similar reasons I am indebted to Dr.
Carlyle King, of the University of Saskatchewan, Saskatoon, who
supervised my master's thesis on Thoreau; and to Dr. A. W.
Plumstead, then of the same university, who encouraged my studies in
this area. A special acknowledgment is due Dr. Walter Harding, of
the State University of New York in Geneseo, whose encouraging response to all my work was a chief incentive for my carrying it through
to completion. I am also grateful to Mary Mahoney-Robson for her
valuable editorial assistance.

I am indebted to the Canada Council for its doctoral fellowships
during the early stages of this study, and for its further aid in the form
of a post-doctoral research grant during the subsequent preparation of
the manuscript.

Finally I wish to acknowledge my debt to the Canadian Federation for
the Humanities, with thanks to Dr. Christopher J. Wernham, Officer,
Aid to Publications Programme, for approving a subvention for my
manuscript. This book has been published with the help of a grant from

the Canadian Federation for the Humanities using funds provided by the Social Sciences and Humanities Research Council of Canada.

My poem, "Thoreau at Walden Pond," has previously appeared in *Thoreau Journal Quarterly*.

Rosthern, Saskatchewan   Victor Carl Friesen

Thoreau at Walden Pond

This is my pond, not mine to own but mine
To know the greatness of—to see the chill,
Gray ghost of dawn evolving from the water,
Or so it seems, and then the sunlit fog
Has curled its vapors from my sight. The pond
Lies new and silver-blue, shaking the sun's
Light in my face.
                        Was that a loon's loud laugh,
Or was the wilderness once crying out
To me? Sometimes I hear, but I don't know
What I have heard (my thoughts were far away),
And then my mind rings clear—but not enough.
Perhaps there is a sound in silence too.
Yet never mind. The pond is fashioned from
The dawn into the day; ducks dive in depths
Of ooze and quack contentedly. I listen—
But there's too much to hear, to hear a thing.

This is my pond, not mine to slip the sleek
Fish from, though I do that at times. The line
I use seems but a cord that fixes me
To nature. Such a tie needs careful tending,
Or the small hold it has may loose itself
And at some superficial joy let go
The small hold altogether.
                        Slowly now
The day fades into night. And soon the pond
In evening lies, a breadth of burnished fire,
With scattered flames against the sky in gold
And green and mauve. And then the gold is gone,
And silver-calm and silhouette have come.
My pond now has more beauty than I see
With mortal eyes. A still merganser slides
His glassy way to sheltered rest. So I
To mine, though I would gladly stay and wait.

1 Up to One's Chin

Thoreau speaks in *Walden* for the "perpetual instilling and drenching of the reality that surrounds us" (II, 107–108). By "reality" he is not thinking of some metaphysical concept in this instance, for he says that he wishes to push past the "alluvion" (II, 108) of philosophy, as well as of religion, poetry, and politics. What he wants to do is to spend one day as deliberately as nature. He can never have enough of nature, we have already noted. "It is essential," he elucidates further in the *Journal*, "that a man confine himself to pursuits which lie next to and conduce to his life. . . . He will confine the observations of his mind as closely as possible to the experience or life of his senses" (XI, 16–17). For Thoreau, the reality he craves must incorporate the experience of a sensuous drenching or immersion in the natural world in which he *at present* is living—whether his role be passive or active, whether the place be forest or shoreline, whether the time be morning or evening, summer or winter. This opening chapter will discuss to what extent such experience pervades his life and writing.

Involvement in the natural world, Thoreau finds, can yield enjoyment for its own sake:

Men tire me when I am not constantly greeted and refreshed as by the flux of sparkling streams. Surely joy is the condition of life. Think of the young fry that leap on ponds, the myriads of insects ushered into being on a summer evening, the incessant note of the hyla with which the woods ring in the spring, the nonchalance of the butterfly carrying accident and change painted in a thousand hues upon its wings, or the brook minnow stoutly stemming the current . . . . (V, 106)

He comments in his *Journal* (XI, 17) that one should dwell as close as possible to the channel in which life flows, and here we find him being immersed in the flux of nature.

Thoreau tries to convey his condition to us with repeated references to motion, a motion taking varied forms and eventually dominating this scene and himself. He refers to a fish which braves the stream, its natural element, while others aggressively jump clear of it. The motion is underlined in that this last action has its parallel on a minute scale in the hatch of tiny insects on the surface — and its contrast in the fluttery course of a larger insect, the butterfly. All the motion points to a related quality, abundant vitality, which he also emphasizes in order to delineate the overwhelming character of the scene. Thus he pictures the fish as young and strong, the butterfly as brilliantly hued, and the frog as persistent and loud of voice. As well, countless numbers of insects are hatched in one evening alone, and Thoreau has successfully created the effect that he as a distinct identity seems to be no longer present, but rather lost in the joyful, chaotic condition of things.

Usually Thoreau's immersion in nature does not completely blot out his identity, however. Instead, he finds himself, as it were, on the boss of the landscape-shield (VII, 13); that is, he is the perceptive center of the tumult in nature encircling him. When this tumult appears diminished so that he seems less involved, he may augment it through his own volition. Thus during the evening quiet on Walden Pond "when . . . he has none to commune with," he strikes the side of his boat with his oar, filling the wooded hills with "circling" sound, "stirring them up as the keeper of a menagerie his wild beasts, until [he] elicit[s] a growl from every wooded vale and hillside" (II, 193). Or he may play his flute and have the charmed perch hover around him. Or, more boisterously, he may fling burning brands into the air, which, like skyrockets, come hissing down into the pond.

Most times Thoreau need but stand motionless to feel immersed in the natural world. Such is the case when he describes the start of his trip on the Concord and Merrimack Rivers. Immediately in the introductory chapter, "Concord River," in the second paragaph, he gives us this description:

Many waves are there agitated by the wind, keeping nature fresh,
the spray blowing in your face, reeds and rushes waving; ducks by
the hundred, all uneasy in the surf, in the raw wind, just ready to
rise, and now going off with a clatter and a whistling like riggers
straight for Labrador, flying against the stiff gale with reefed wings,
or else circling round first, with all their paddles briskly moving,
just over the surf, to reconnoiter you before they leave these parts;
gulls wheeling overhead, muskrats swimming for dear life, wet and
cold, with no fire to warm them by that you know of, their labored
homes rising here and there like haystacks; and countless mice and
moles and winged titmice along the sunny, windy shore; cranberries
tossed on the waves and heaving up on the beach, their little red
skiffs beating about among the alders; — such healthy natural tumult
. . . . (I, 5)

Here, as in the passage which speaks of joy surely being the condition
of life, there is a great deal of movement. The verb phrase, "are . . .
agitated ," effectively sets the tone, for it can apply not only to wind
and water but to the ducks, uneasy to be off, and to the muskrats
swimming for dear life. The length itself of the description helps to
convey this sense of "healthy natural tumult," but in this passage
Thoreau seems to be caught up in it. Although he uses the second person "you" in order to involve the reader in his experience, it is
Thoreau about whom the ducks are circling round, reconnoitering, increasing the sense of his being enwrapped in the natural world. In a
kind of variation on the pathetic fallacy, he refers to the "red skiffs" of
cranberries which beat about on the waves, thereby suggesting their
affinity to him in that they anticipate his own coming journey. And
with the spray blowing into his face, he, in a sense, has been an-
nointed, has received nature's blessing for his undertaking. Thus he
ends the introductory chapter with the idea of becoming part of
nature's flux: "I resolved to launch myself on [the river's] bosom and
float whither it would bear me" (I, 11).

The passage depicting nature's "healthy . . . tumult" is in the present tense, as if Thoreau is experiencing his sensuous immersion in
nature now, but particularly noteworthy is that most of the verb
forms, some dozen of them, are in the progressive tense as well, ending

in *ing*. There is a suggestion of a continuing present, an extension of one moment into an eternity which precludes past and future. It is typical of Thoreau to wish to concentrate everything into one grand moment, and so he says elsewhere that the whole duty of life concerns the question of how to respire and aspire both at once (VII, 300). This feeling, combined with his sensuousness, leads to another dictum: "We live but a fraction of our life. Why do we not let on the flood, raise the gates, and set all our wheels in motion? He that hath ears to hear, let him hear. Employ your senses" (VIII, 251). With a Biblical reference to ears and hearing, Thoreau not only gives added sanction to his concluding three-word injunction but also, by means of a pun, wishes to be understood literally. We should, in fact, use our ears — and our other senses too.

Using one's senses means living now. There is no other life the like of this, Thoreau believes. In *Walden* he says: "I have been anxious . . . to stand on the meeting of two eternities, the past and future, which is precisely the present moment; to toe that line" (II, 18). In his *Journal* he shows that this is exactly the position of constituents of the natural world — and he equates his life with theirs: "My life as essentially belongs to the present as that of a willow tree in the spring. Now, now its catkins expand, its yellow bark shines, its sap flows" (VIII, 232). In another entry he ungrammatically emphasizes the verb *to be* in describing his own situation: "over all, myself and condition is and does" (VII, 190). We should note that *to be* — with its corresponding first-person affirmation, *I am* — is something complete in itself: no object need follow the verb. In Thoreau's awkward sentence the verb "is" completes the thought (it takes no object), while the other verb, "does," suggests a timeless continuum. Stasis — his insistence on the present moment — has obliterated past and future.

Indeed, Thoreau's love of the present world leads him to criticize Christianity, as he then sees it. Either it dwells upon the past — "It has dreamed a sad dream, and does not yet welcome the morning with joy" (I, 78) — and so its adherents fail to respond sensuously to the day here and now; or else it in radical fashion directs its thoughts to a future world when his senses tell him that this world is heaven enough. "Talk of heaven! ye disgrace earth" (II, 222); "Olympus is but the outside of this earth everywhere" (II, 99). In contrast, he commends the Hindu religion for preaching the custom of *timeless* gods. It is a "sublime conservatism" (I, 140). "We should be blessed," he says in *Walden*, "if we lived in the present always" (II, 346).

Thoreau would prefer to be blessed no more in a Hindu mosque than in a Christian cathedral. However, one of the few such structures he can admire is Montreal's Notre Dame Cathedral during his Yankee visit to Canada and only then because he feels that he is inside a great cave in the midst of a city. It is as if he were enveloped in his beloved outdoor world once again. The "cathedral" he prefers is a natural one consisting of groves of various trees. Thus in the opening paragraph of the "Baker Farm" chapter of *Walden*, he speaks of pines "standing like temples . . . , so soft and green and shady that Druids would have forsaken their oaks to worship in them"; of cedars "fit to stand before Valhalla"; of white spruces under which toadstools are "round tables of the swamp gods"; and of a hemlock "standing like a pagoda" (II, 223–224). Thoreau's references here to several religions of East and West make these groves a universal cathedral, and these are the shrines, he tells us, which he visits summer and winter.[1]

Thoreau's reason for seeking them appears obvious from a closer examination of this paragraph. Immersed in the woods, he finds much to appeal to the senses. Both the black and yellow birch there, he says, are "perfumed": they contribute to the total woodland fragrance. The sense of sight is gratified by the wavy pine boughs, "rippling with light," or by the beech tree, "beautifully lichen-painted, perfect in all its details." Other treats for his eye are the hoary blue berries covering the cedar and the lichen festooning the spruce, while at his feet there are fungi adorning the stumps, "like butterflies or shells." On the forest floor too are swamp-pink and dogwood growing and also the red alder berry. His sense of taste begins to be gratified by the mere presence of this wild berry and of others, which, he says, dazzle and tempt him. He terms them "forbidden fruits, too fair for mortal taste," and so his woodland cathedral changes into a primal Eden.

When Thoreau is immersed in a real primitive wood, in Maine, he exclaims joyfully: "What a place to live, what a place to die and be buried in!" In this instance he has just been enumerating the sensuous qualities of this forest, and these offset for him the stern aspects of wilderness. Here for eye, tongue, and extended foot are silver birches, insipid berries, and moss-grown rocks. For the ear are the notes of chickadee and woodpecker, laugh of loon, cry of osprey and eagle, whistle of ducks, and hooting of owl. All these sensations give the grim forest an "inexpressible tenderness" (III, 89–90). It is with this feeling that he can write elsewhere: "Such is the genialness of nature that the trees appear to have put out feelers by which our senses apprehend them more tenderly" (XVIII, 32).

This kind of sensuous involvement can take two related forms for Thoreau: a feeling that he is part of the woodland world or a feeling that that world is part of him. The first response is well expressed in a passage from the *Lost Journal*: "I love to look aslant up the tree tops from some dell, and finally rest myself in the blueish mistiness of the white pines" (*LJ*, 187).[2] The second response may be exemplified by a sentence which refers to his second excursion to the Maine woods: "For my dessert, I helped myself to a large slice of the Chesuncook woods, and took a hearty draught of its waters with all my senses" (III, 143). The two responses are significant not only because they are in effect opposite to each other and so point to his wide-ranging approach to nature but also because they show the poles of his thinking with regard to man's importance relative to nature, a subject to be fully discussed in Chapter 8. If it seems at times as though nature is sought as a kind of enveloping maternal security (he after all addresses it consistently as "she," adopting the convention that it is *Mother* Nature of whom he is speaking[3]), his healthy sensuous appetite dictates his wish to be "immersed" inwardly as well as outwardly. The kind of "shelter" he seeks in nature is not so much protective as it is that kind found under a cloud (II, 230), for he welcomes all sensuous experiences in the outdoor world. His philosophy is that "when a dog runs at you, [you should] whistle for him" (VII, 153).

Thoreau's sense of being immersed in the outdoor world, inwardly and outwardly, applies as much, and perhaps more obviously, to nature's seas and rivers as to nature's woodlands. When he bathes in the local river and says that he "would fain be the channel of a mountain brook" (VIII, 335), then he wants the watery element to be part of him. His wish is the same when he writes at another time: "I must let the water soak into me" (XII, 383). But when he states that he wants to mingle himself with the waters of a pond, then it is an immersion outwardly that he craves. In either case he exults in the physical pleasure of the experience.

While at Cape Cod, Thoreau confronts the sea in similar fashion. He may walk along the shore, "determined to get the sea into [him]" (IV, 177); that is, determined to appreciate its essence by perceiving it with all his senses, just as he did the waters of the Chesuncook woods. Or, conversely, he may actually immerse himself in the salty waters. His delight with this last experience is increased by the sight of fish against polished stones and a sandy bottom and by the touch of seaweed: "The bottom being sandy, I could see the sea-perch swimming about. The smooth and fantastically worn rocks, and the perfectly clean and tress-like rock-weeds falling over you, and attached so firmly to the rocks that you could pull yourself up by them, greatly enhanced . . . the bath" (IV, 16).

Perhaps Thoreau's greatest sense of immersion in nature occurs in that kind of topography which combines the features of forest and water, that is, in a swamp. "Such a depth of verdure into which you sink" (X, 281), he exclaims in one journal passage. In another he states that when we have no "appetite" and life has lost its "flavor," then the *solution* is to enter a swamp (X, 231) [my pun, although Thoreau would approve]. In yet another journal entry he comments on the amount and the various kinds of life found there—swimming muskrats, splashing turtles, cat-o'-nine-tails, and good cranberries—much to gratify the senses. The journal passage most representative of his sensuous feeling for a swamp is that which he later incorporates in *A Week*:

I can fancy that it would be a luxury to stand up to one's chin in some retired swamp a whole summer day, scenting the wild honeysuckle and bilberry blows, and lulled by the minstrelsy of gnats and mosquitoes! A day passed in the society of those Greek sages, such as described in the *Banquet* of Xenophon, would not be comparable with the dry wit of decayed cranberry vines, and the fresh Attic salt of the moss beds. Say twelve hours of genial and familiar converse with the leopard frog; the sun to rise behind alder and dogwood, and climb buoyantly to his meridian of two hands' breadth, and finally sink to rest behind some bold western hummock. To hear the evening chant of the mosquito from a thousand green chapels, and the bittern begin to boom from some concealed fort like a sunset gun! Surely one may as profitably be soaked in the juices of a swamp for one day as pick his way dry-shod over sand. Cold and damp,—are they not as rich experience as warmth and dryness? (I, 319–320).

Here is something for all the senses: flowers to smell, insects and a bird to hear, wild fruit to taste, the sun's progress to watch, and the "juices" of the swamp to feel.

That Thoreau wishes to stand in the swamp "up to [his] chin" is significant. It is not complete immersion (in nature) that he desires, at least not continuously, but only to that extent that his thinking self, the protruding head, is free to have a *conscious* appreciation of the surrounding scene.[4] Thus, for only a portion of the description does he seem to be more or less one with the swampy world, and that occurrence follows the familiar converse with the frog. At that time he takes a frog's-eye view of things—sees the sun sink behind the frog's skyline of tussocks and hears its mortal antagonist, the bittern, as an enemy announcing his presence with a cannon blast. Meanwhile, the frog's own prey, the mosquitoes, appear to seek supplication in their green chapels of grass. But even this part of the description consists of a conscious, deliberate prose which shows that Thoreau has not become completely amphibious. He is like those frogs which he has described earlier in this same book as "meditating, . . . summing up their week, with one eye out on the golden sun, and one toe upon a reed, eying the wondrous universe in which they act their part" (I, 48). The frogs are both "acting" their role in nature and "eying" in a knowing way. Thoreau is both soaking up the juices of the swamp just by his presence there and also knowingly contrasting this activity with listening to the wit of Greek sages—and note his priority. One may assume that while he is in the swamp, he wants to cherish the present moment; prefers it for the time being to anything else. And yet he speaks of being there for but "one" summer day. He must leave the swamp for the same reason that he leaves Walden Pond: there are other lives to live, or, in this case, other things sensuously to enjoy. The final sentence of the passage may be reversed: cold and damp *are* rich experiences but so are warmth and dryness.

Every day is rich in sensuous experiences for Thoreau—from early morning when after a "partial cessation of . . . sensuous life" man's sense organs are revitalized (II, 99)—to late evening "when the whole body is one sense, and imbibes delight through every pore" (II, 143). The morning he describes as a time of "teeming air" (XII, 285) because the atmosphere seems many-chambered, full of infinite sounds. The hearing of one of those sounds, a sparrow's song, can be the event of a whole forenoon (III, 249). The afternoon is a time when he keeps his studio hours. His "work" may be nothing more than what he indicates in this comment—"My errand this afternoon was chiefly to look at the gooseberry at Saw Mill Brook" (XII, 257)—but it is important to him. The approach of night begins with sunset, and this he describes as the "most gorgeous sight in nature!" Life is too grand then to be eating supper; he must be outdoors and looking westward. He sees before him in the sky a phantom city "over whose pavements the horses of the sun have already hurried" (VIII, 296), and he wanders those streets in his imagination. During night itself he is not content to glimpse the moon only through a crack in a shutter. "Why not walk a little in her light?" he asks (V, 324). It is at such time that every plant, he tells us, emits its odor, from swamp-pink growing in a meadow to tansy along a road, and rills meanwhile sound clearly which he had not detected before.

Something sensuous is gained too by experiencing all kinds of weather. A "washing" day, as Thoreau describes it, is a good time for him since the atmosphere is clear, sounds carry far, and the air smells sweet. On a dark "mizzling" day, on the other hand, he finds that, huddled against the rain, he is "all compact," open to impressions. He is compelled to look at nearby objects and finds that nearby sounds are magnified: the mist is "like a roof and walls over and around" (XIV, 14).[5] He thoroughly enjoys being out in the rain: "You wander indefinitely in a beaded coat, wet to the skin of your legs, sit on moss-clad rocks and stumps, and hear the lisping of migrating sparrows . . . . The part of you that is wettest is fullest of life, like the lichens . . . . You glide along the distant wood-side, full of joy and expectation, seeing nothing but beauty, hearing nothing but music . . . " (XVI, 262–263). And a stormy day to him is "cheerful" (X, 318) because that is how he himself feels when he is "weather-beaten" (XVIII, 26). He feels exuberant also because of what can be perceived then: "A life of fair-weather walks *might* never show you the goose sailing over our waters, or the great heron feeding here" (IX, 444).

As individual days are rich in sensuous esperiences, so are individual seasons, not just the summertime when it is luxurious to stand immersed in a swamp. True, Thoreau says that he tends to lay up a stock of sensations in summer as a squirrel does nuts, but he wishes to imbibe whatever nutriment each season has for him. Thus, he tells us, he gives himself up to nature: "live in each season as it passes; breathe the air, drink the drink, taste the fruit, and resign yourself to the influences of each. Let them be your only diet drink . . . . Be blown on by all the winds. Open all your pores and bathe in all the tides of Nature, in all her streams and oceans, at all seasons" (XI, 394). Again, he wishes to be immersed inwardly, as though nature were a medicine to be swallowed in large draughts, and to be engulfed outwardly, as though it also were an immense, unlimited flux.

The winter season finds Thoreau once more in the swamp, immersed not in its waters but in its covering snows: "I love to wade and flounder through [it] now, these bitter cold days when the snow lies deep on the ground" (XIV, 99). Elsewhere he speaks of winter in these terms of sensuous involvement: "the snow blows right merrily in [one's] face" (IV, 41); "it is invigorating to breathe the . . . air, ... and we would fain stay out long and late, that the gales may sigh through us, too, as through the leafless trees, and fit us for the winter" (V, 167). Winter is a "grand old poem" (XV, 167) to be read with all the senses.

In spring Thoreau is outdoors again, and to him, nothing is more affecting than the sight of bare soil, for man is a child of the earth: "It is a good collyrium to look on [it], — to pore over it so much, getting strength to all your senses, like Antaeus" (XVIII, 89). This time he is enveloped in the fragrant exhalation of the thawing earth: "the sun dispersing the mist smiles on a checkered landscape of russet and white smoking with incense, through which [one] picks his way from islet to islet, cheered by the music of a thousand tinkling rills and rivulets" (II, 336). "Incense" not only has a sensuous connotation but a religious one as well. He seems to suggest that he as the person within the rising "incense," immersed in the world of spring, has divine favor.

It is in the season following summer that Thoreau's wish to be immersed in the outdoor world (with of course an awareness of such immersion) is perhaps most apparent. In his essay, "Autumnal Tints," he is up to his chin in reds and scarlets and oranges and yellows as he describes the countryside in fall. The account is a kind of Keatsian prose tribute to autumn, outrivaling the ode of the poet in its accumulating of, and expanding upon, the warm colors of the season. We sense Thoreau's absorption in this world when he describes himself standing under several drooping trees in their yellow foliage: "it is as if I stood within a ripe pumpkin-rind, and I feel as mellow as if I were the pulp" (V, 236). In another instance the autumn colors prompt a sensuous gratification other than visual: "I cut [a pokewood] for a cane, for I would fain handle and lean on it. I love to press the berries between my fingers, and see their juice staining my hand. To walk amid those upright, branching casks of purple wine, which retain and diffuse a sunset glow, tasting each one with your eye . . . , what a privilege!" (V, 255).

In each season the terrain underfoot is always different. In fall, Thoreau walks through piles of dried leaves, making, according to Channing, as much noise as possible; winter presents him with frosted evergreens, and to walk amid them is to hear his feet "cronch" them as if he were "walking through the cellar of some confectioner to the gods" (X, 441); in spring, he is thrilled to walk again on naked earth; while in summer, he describes a walk in the river in these terms: "Now your feet expand on a smooth sandy bottom, now contract timidly on pebbles, now slump in genial fatty mud—greasy, saponaceous—amid the pads" (X, 220).

Such sauntering through the seasons is an indulgence of the five senses, but the descriptions are also the chief paradigm in his work of kinesthetic sensuousness—an awareness of the sensations in one's skin, muscles, and joints that proceed from a voluntary motion of the body.[6] In his descriptions here the sensations arise not merely in sympathetic correspondence to the bodily movements of some wild creature, as is the case with the "dancing" squirrel referred to later in Chapter 5, but from his own actions, his own participation, as it were, in the processes of nature. Indulging his kinesthetic sense—feeling dried leaves, hoarfrost, bare earth, or riverbed underfoot and feeling also the muscles work in legs and feet as he adjusts his stride for each "terrain"—he experiences the world in a simple, primitive fashion.

Thoreau has learned early in boyhood the delight of steeping himself in such sensations. "See, hear, smell, taste, . . . while these senses are fresh and pure" (VIII, 330), he advises, and he has lived up to his advice. If with increasing age his senses do not retain their original clarity, this loss is compensated for by his diligent use of them.[7] We know that his eyesight deteriorates, but he assures us that his hearing actually improves over the years. By keeping his chin, and mind, above water (in the swamp of nature, while still being immersed in its element), he never loses the delight of living a sensuous life. He becomes infatuated with the earth. Once we are possessed with an idea of something, he tells us, we can hardly see anything else, and so it is with his infatuation. He is obsessed with "lov[ing] the crust of the earth on which [he] dwell[s] more than the sweet crust or any bread or cake" (XVI, 258). In another instance, he says: "I love nature, I love the landscape. . . . it is cheerfully, musically earnest" (VIII, 100).

"I love," we see, is a frequent beginning to sentences in the *Journal*, as Thoreau again and again expresses his love for those things which stimulate the senses. No sense is slighted: sight—"*I love* to see a sandy road . . . curving through a pitch pine wood" (IX, 405); sound—"*I love* to hear the wind howl" (IX, 408); smell—"*I love* the sweet fragrance of meliot" (X, 219); taste—"*I love* to drink the water of the meadow or the river I pass the day on" (X, 170); and touch—"*I love* to sit on the withered grass" (XII, 486) [my italics]. In the rhetoric he uses, his love of being "drenched" by the surrounding world may resemble a pupil's affection for his studies—or resemble the appetite of a hungry man for food, as has been already suggested—or resemble Antaeus's needful love of the earth—or resemble the relation between lovers—or, most likely, resemble a combination of all these. He speaks of thumbing nature as if she were an old spelling book. He sees the earth as a huge fruit which he must press with his knee to hear if it does not crack with ripeness. He both lies and relies on the earth, he tells us in one of his many puns (VIII, 100). He can hug the earth for joy; all nature is his bride. Always he counts himself among those who cherish the present condition of things with the enthusiasm of a lover. His feeling for the sensate world will be even more evident in a specific consideration of his use of each sense.

2 A Body All Sentient

Thoreau writes: "A man should feed his senses with the best that the land affords" (VIII, 496). The best for him means "what his senses hourly perceive," the "commonest events, every-day phenomena." From these he derives his "satisfaction" (XIV, 204). The acuity of Thoreau's senses as they perceive such phenomena and his pervasive use of each sense show just how satisfactory his life in nature is.

Thoreau's five senses seem to be particularly acute. He tells us, for example, of his awareness of the subtle blending of waning sunlight and evening moonlight as the latter, "shedding the softest imaginable light," gains prominence with the end of day. "What an immeasurable interval there is," he writes, "between the first tinge of moonlight which we detect, lighting with mysterious, silvery, poetic light the western slopes, like a paler grass, and the last wave of sunlight on the eastern slopes! It is wonderful how our senses ever span so vast an interval, how from being aware of one we become aware of the other" (VIII, 284).

This last sentence hints at three reasons for the acuteness of Thoreau's senses. First, we might ordinarily assume that the phenomenon of changing light is strictly a matter of vision, but not to Thoreau. He speaks of senses spanning the interval and elsewhere tells how senses other than sight "serve, and escort, and defend it" (*LJ*, 165). Here he detects the changes in light not only through the eye but through the ear as well, for "already the crickets chirp to the moon a different strain" (VIII, 284). Secondly, his perception throughout the "interval" seems attentive and continuous. He disciplines himself to sense all that he can. "Objects are concealed from our view," he writes elsewhere, "not so much because they are out of the course of our visual ray (continued) as because there is no intention of the mind and eye toward them" (XVII, 285). Thirdly, he says that awareness of one phenomenon prompts his awareness of another. He may mean that one phenomenon accentuates the other by contrast—however slight the difference may be in this instance of sunlight and moonlight. Or he may mean that his being aware of the first phenomenon causes him to anticipate the second. He is ready to perceive it. Both effects are important to his sensuous approach to nature.

Both effects, we find, are referred to in his essay "Autumnal Tints." There he states that the colors of autumn would not be so effective were it not for the contrast provided by evergreens. And he concludes the essay with an extended image on anticipation of nature's beauty. The sensuous man here becomes a hunter with a gun who shoots this beauty, not by firing random shots into the sky but by taking "particular aim" and knowing what he is aiming at. He knows the seasons and haunts of his game bird, "the color of its wing"; "trains himself, dresses and watches unweariedly"; and finally "wades in water up to his knees, . . . and *therefore* he gets it." He has "*anticipate*[d] it" [Thoreau's italics] and so can flush it at every step (V, 287–288).

Many times Thoreau refers to the acuteness of his senses in terms of his anticipation and/or training. Consider his visual sense first. While in the Maine woods, he notes that the river he is on is an inclined plane, for he observes the water line against the shores. His companion does not perceive the slope, we are told, not having Thoreau's experience as a surveyor. The very last entry in the *Journal*, made when Thoreau was already dying of tuberculosis, continues in a similar vein. He notices furrows made by the rain, "all . . . perfectly distinct to an observant eye, and yet could easily pass unnoticed by most" (XX, 346). But he also has eyesight acute in itself. In the Maine woods he sees a dragonfly half a mile distant; at Walden Pond he sees a water bug dimple the surface a quarter mile away. Sensitive to color, he can detect sassafras from as great a distance as half a mile because of its peculiar orange-scarlet tint. And one winter day, in midafternoon, he discerns a star in the skies overhead. Truly he has said that his eyes are flocks, roaming about the far mountains and sky and feeding on them.

Thoreau's sense of hearing is no less acute than his sense of sight — and for similar reasons. He has trained his ears both to distinguish slight sounds — he hears not only the cluck after a whippoorwill's note, but as well a fly-like buzzing — and to be anticipatory of them. Thus he has no need to go to the world of fine arts for music but can hear music in the simplest sounds, from the humming of telegraph wires to the clicking of oarlocks. Even the silence of night is to him audible and "something positive." "It is musical and thrills me," he writes (X, 471–472).[1]

The acuity of Thoreau's other senses is also noteworthy. His sense of smell, by his own account, is a much perfected sense, akin to that of an animal. When, for instance, he lands on an island in the Sudbury River, he notices at once the scent of wilted leaves, presumably learning thereby something of their life history. That he chooses to record this one sensation shows how significant it must be to him. Significant also is the first appearance of muskrats in the spring, and he *smells* their presence. On one occasion he smells a fox's scent from a trail that must have been at least twelve hours old. Another sense, that of taste, Thoreau seems to regard as inferior to the other senses, calling it "commonly gross" (II, 241), but we may be sure that if use and anticipation, again, develop acuteness, his sense of taste is perceptive enough. On his walks he is constantly nibbling from the plants about him and making comparisons. Furthermore, he lives on the simplest foods, keeping his taste unjaded. His fifth sense, the sense of touch, is well developed like the others. When climbing a hill, he detects the different temperatures of the air strata he passes through, and on a hill itself he suggests that he feels even the "atoms" (VII, 13) of wind, that is, its minute constituents, touching his cheek. He writes elsewhere: "My body is all sentient. As I go here or there, I am tickled by this or that I come in contact with, as if I touched the wires of a battery. I can generally recall — have fresh in my mind — several scratches last received. These I constantly recall to mind, reimpress, and harp upon" (XIV, 44).

If his body is all sentient, Thoreau does attach some superiority to one of the senses — the sense of sight — and it will be given detailed consideration first. He holds it foremost because with it he can detect color and form. It is color that stains the windows in the cathedral of his world

(IX, 442). He finds it the "more glorious" to live in his native Concord because one of its birds, the common blue jay, is "so splendidly painted" (XVII, 319). Thoreau, we see, in spite of his response to the subtleties of color, does not neglect the obvious. His heart leaps up at the sight of a rainbow; he devotes a separate essay to the beauty of trees in autumn. In this essay he speaks of seeing another brilliantly colored bird, the wood duck, afloat in a pool covered with fallen leaves, also brilliantly hued. He makes no comment about his own reaction, but he ends his statement with an exclamation point. His captivation by the scene is to be understood. In the *Journal* he is more explicit about the colors of the wood duck and the effect on him: "What an ornament to a river to see that glowing gem floating in contact with the water! As if the hummingbird should recline its ruby throat and its breast on the water. Like dipping a glowing coal in water! It so affected me" (XIV, 17). It is the contrast here which enhances the picture for him.

Thoreau's response to warm colors, such as red, is somewhat different from his response to cool tints, such as blue — the two broad groups of colors which contrast most vividly with each other. The associations he makes with each of them go beyond the actual functioning of his sense of sight but tell us something which he considers important — the effect of this one sense on his total being. We feel that his response, even though it is for the most part conventional, is highly personal too because of the emotion with which he expresses it. Warm colors for him are summery and speak of the earth, and he appropriately reacts warmly to them; whereas cool colors tend to be wintry and associated with things of the heavens, something to be reflective about.

Of the warm colors, red is Thoreau's favorite: he loves to see any redness in vegetation (VIII, 489). It is the color of colors, he says in "Autumnal Tints," and speaks to our blood. His use of the term "blood" in relation to the effect of the color on our vital principle and/or physical nature is apt because the term can also suggest heroism, as in battles fought, and fruition, as in maturity and ripeness attained, and both suggestions are developed in the essay. The oaks described there look "like soldiers in red" (V, 283) while the maple is "like one great scarlet fruit full of ripe juices, every leaf" (V, 259). Red foliage, he says elsewhere, shows nature as being "full of blood and heat and luxuriance" (VIII, 490). In his enthusiasm over this color, he shows us his own reaction more directly when he describes a scarlet tanager. Even when he knows the bird is present, the sudden appearance of the "bloody fellow" always "startle[s]" him; that "incredible" red "transport[s]" him; it "enhances" the wildness (XI, 187). Other warm colors too, such as yellows and oranges, are something to feast one's eyes on, although Thoreau realizes that he can revel in them because they are not the staple of his diet. Thus he writes of yet another warm color but one sober in its aspect: "Brown is the color for me, the color of our coats and our daily lives, the color of the poor man's loaf. The bright tints are pies and cakes, good only for October feasts" (XVIII, 97–98).

Thoreau is also rapturous at times about cool blues and azures, but these tints, found predominantly in the sky above and in the waters which reflect it, are often wedded to meditation, just as the blue Pacific was to Herman Melville's Ishmael. There is a sense of limitless space suggested by these colors to Thoreau and also accompanying far-reaching thoughts about his own make-up. The notion of distancing is apparent in two references from *Walden*. He speaks of a faraway ridge made "interesting" to his eyes by the "azure tint" the intervening atmosphere imparts to it (II, 136) and of "still bluer and more distant mountain ranges in the northwest, those true-blue coins from heaven's own mint" (II, 96). The blue mountains are associated not with the earth but "heaven," that is, with things ethereal.

In the *Journal* a similar association made with this color causes Thoreau to reflect about the nature of his own being: "I think I never saw a more elysian blue than my shadow [on the winter's snow]. I am turned into a tall blue Prussian from my cap to my boots, such as no mortal dye can produce, with an amethystine hatchet in my hand. I am in raptures at my own shadow. What if the substance were of as ethereal a nature?" (XIV, 115). Of course, his *spiritual* substance is this very thing, and it is fitting, then, that in the season where the coolest "color" of all predominates — winter with its whiteness when "the waters become solid and ma[k]e a sky below" (XIII, 141) — he plumbs the depths of Walden Pond and, symbolically, the depths of his own soul. Curiously enough, when he envisions the color of his soul in *A*

Week, it is not white but a "bright invisible green" (I, 250). "Invisible" does suggest an absence of color, as in white, but he has named a tint which also can be part of either the warm or cool spectra. It is a characteristic color of a winter sky and of springtime growth. It is a halfway color, and the essence of Thoreau, his life-giving principle, is apparently as much of the earth as of heaven.

In recording the colors of his world, Thoreau notices what would be commonly overlooked by others. He sees the gem-like play of colors of fungi on a stump and notices too the irridescence left on a patch of water by a decaying sucker. To him the irridescence is like the "fragments of a most wonderfully painted mirror" (XIV, 343), and he leans over the edge of his boat, admiring it as much as he would a sunset sky or rainbow. Often he goes out of his way—indeed such going becomes his way of life—to notice particular colors in nature. He walks an extra half mile to examine the changing colors of a tree; he wades through cold water in order to gaze at cranberries. But he seems to go out of his way most frequently in winter when the landscape is less vivid than in other seasons. One day, with a temperature of six below zero, finds him pacing up and down a road, waiting until the light is right: he wants to observe the pinkish cast on a snowy hill at sunset. After the moment has passed, he discerns as well a delicate violet tinge on the hill (XVII, 395–396). Another evening he notices the rose color of the snow and "*at the same time*" (he italicizes this last phrase) notices a greenish hue in nearby ice, having, as he says, been looking out for such coincidence (XIX, 61).

Thoreau's writings include many accounts of his sitting at some vantage point, letting his eye sweep over the natural scene before him in order to distinguish each color. This is one way of "harvesting an annual crop with [his] eyes" (XVII, 77) from sky, water, and woods. It is a luxury, he tells us, to let his eye rest on a mackerel sky, noting the different hues from zenith to horizon. Perhaps the best known instance where he gives a sweeping look at water occurs in "The Ponds" chapter of *Walden* (II, 196), an activity which he later describes as a "soothing employment" (II, 208). Elsewhere, his eye sweeps over a river— "[it] is divided into five portions—first the weedy and padded borders, than a smooth, silvery stripe, . . . and next the blue rippled portion, succeeded by the broader silver, and the pads of the eastern side" (XVII, 84) — and sweeps over the sea — it is "green, or greenish, as some ponds; then blue for many miles, often with purple tinges, bounded in the distance by a light silvery stripe; beyond which there is generally a dark-blue rim" (IV, 119).

In these illustrations Thoreau's eye has been surveying more or less flat surfaces, and his response tends to be merely enumerative, a listing of succeeding colors. But when his eye sweeps over woodlands, moving, as he says in *Walden*, "by just gradations from the low shrubs . . . to the highest trees" (II, 206), then his eye seems tactile in also sensing the *texture* of the scene. Thus the shrubby hill and swamp country of Cape Cod is like the "richest rug imaginable," matchless by the work of any dye *or* loom. The "lowness and thickness of the shrubbery, no less than the brightness of the tints" contribute to the uniqueness of this landscape. He does list the colors of each shrub but must add that each "mak[es] its own figure" (IV, 193–195). In a similar fashion he is concerned with decorative effect, not only with regard to color but with regard to space, when he describes a shoreline scene of various flowers in *A Week*. In his description the many individual colors seem to be carefully positioned in relationship to each other. They lie "in front," "on either hand," "on the margin," and "sprinkled here and there" (I, 18). The effect, we can say, is that of a Matisse painting, where decorative arrangement is such a telling feature.

Thoreau's eye is as sensitive to forms and outlines in nature as to colors. He detects the earth's muscles in leafless tree limbs (XVII, 260) and in firm, curving beaches (XVIII, 75), while flowing waters and swaying foliage are the wrists and temple of the earth (XIX, 138). He can feel their pulse with his eye. "A man has not seen a thing who has not felt it," he says (XIX, 160). Seeing for him becomes something which is not distinct from either outward (tactile) feeling or from inward feelings. Both kinds of feeling are evident when he devotes three pages of "Autumnal Tints" to the form of an oak leaf. "What a wild and pleasing outline, a combination of graceful curves and angles!" (V, 279) he exclaims over it. He first treats the leaf anatomically, referring to its broad sinuses or long lobes. But his enthusiasm over its form prompts him to find another descriptive image, this one geographical. The leaf is an island or a pond with rounded bays and pointed capes, and he becomes a mariner at sight of it. It is like a miniature

Walden Pond, whose scalloped shoreline he also loves to follow with his eye (II, 206).

When leaves are more distant, that is, still on a tree above him, Thoreau is pleased to see their shapes enhanced because of the bright sky behind them. The leaves then "grasp . . . skyey influences" (V, 278) or stamp their meaning "in a thousand hieroglyphics on the heavens" (I, 166). The outline of them gains in richness for him as the number of interstices increases through which the light straggles. More border is thus provided along which his eye can travel with what amounts really to a caress. Pines, he can say, make a "graceful fringe to the earth" (I, 167), while elsewhere he notes that his eyes "nibble the piny sierra which makes the horizon's edge, as a hungry man nibbles a cracker" (XVII, 450).

The features of a natural scene often seem to Thoreau like the components of a picture, and this awareness in turn affects how he will continue to see the scene. The atmosphere and trees present not a kind of screen to gaze at but the glass and frame of a painting. In *A Week* he says at one place that the "air was so elastic and crystalline that it had the same effect on the landscape that a glass has on a picture, to give it an ideal remoteness and perfection" (I, 45). And in "Autumnal Tints" he refers to the sunset painted daily behind a frame of elms, making a picture worthier than any found in a gallery. Such a frame can serve several purposes. In this case the trees, by contrast, bring out the red colors of the western sky. Other uses are suggested elsewhere in his writings.

When in *The Maine Woods* he speaks of glimpsing the expanse of a concealed lake through a narrow opening of trees, the trees really accentuate his sense of the panorama lying behind them. In the *Journal* meanwhile, Thoreau says that if we would enjoy a prospect, we should look from the edge of a plateau, with the plateau "seen as the lower frame of a picture," in order to give the view greater depth (XX, 40). Such is his experience in the New Hampshire hills where, through a gap, he catches sight of a ship in full sail, "over a field of corn, twenty or thirty miles at sea" (I, 191). He compares the effect to that of seeing a slide of a painted ship being passed through a magic lantern. On another occasion when he sees a woodchopper close at hand "through a vista between two trees," the man appears "with the same distinctness as objects seen through a pinhole in a card" (IX, 254). The natural frame in this instance appears to have dwarfed the man's size so that, although "charmingly distinct," he seems ideal rather than actual. Thoreau comments that a recognition of this kind of effect has perhaps led some men to be painters.

An eighteenth-century landscape painter and writer, William Gilpin, whose works on Picturesque beauty Thoreau read, probably caused Thoreau to look for certain beauties in nature which he might not otherwise have noticed so soon. Thoreau, wishing to make his visual sense serve him to the fullest, was only too willing to learn from other observers. Thus he writes to a friend that Gilpin's books have been his thunder lately. After reading the artist's *Forest Scenery*, he writes in his *Journal*, "The mist to-day makes those near distances which Gilpin tells of" (IX, 444), or "Thinking of the value of the gull to the scenery of our river in spring . . . , [I find that] Gilpin says something to the purpose" (IX, 416).[2] It is as if Thoreau were looking at the landscape afresh, through the eyes of a painter. In another journal entry Thoreau's description of an autumn scene (XX, 89) is reminiscent of a Gilpin painting: a shining stream framed by shrubbery, the horizon blurred by smoke, clouds billowing upwards, man and his works seeming insignificant against a panorama of nature. All this is seen by him in a downward perspective from a railroad causeway.

It should not be thought that Thoreau is here permeated by aesthetic ideas of the late eighteenth century. For one thing, he, as sensuous man, generally wants to be central (and significant) in the richly satisfying world about him. (The final chapter discusses this point.) He is unlike, then, another British artist of the period, Richard Wilson, whose style is similar to Gilpin's in depicting grand scenery, or the nature poet James Thomson, whose *The Seasons*, 1730, portrays man as inconsequential before the forces of nature. If anything, Thoreau is akin to Jane Austen, who in *Sense and Sensibility*, 1811, dramatizes the pros and cons of Picturesque ideas and clearly speaks for the gentle and the familiar in landscape rather than the "sublime."[3] According to Edmund Burke's *The Sublime and the Beautiful*, 1756, the sublime features of nature, those of great magnitude, produce sensations of pain and terror. Influential artists like Gilpin were preoccupied in experiencing such scenes and having viewers experience them in their paintings. But Thoreau's one excursion into sublime scenery, up Mount Katahdin, makes him prefer his own native Concord, although he does not regret the climb. (The following chapter considers the episode fully.)

For another thing, Thoreau is not concerned primarily with a romantically Picturesque view but with a view of as much nature, in all its variety, as possible. At Walden he stands on tiptoe when looking at his horizons. Gilpin looks at nature with only the eye of an artist, and Thoreau criticizes him for doing so. Nature is more than near distances and side screens and backdrops to Thoreau. It is a living thing, like himself, which he wants to respond to with his whole being, not just with the sense of sight but with the other senses as well.

If Thoreau does not already see acutely enough, the hearing of a cricket, he tells us, whets his eyes. Sound to him can be as exhilarating as color and form. It is "coincident with an ecstasy" (XII, 39), and he devotes a whole chapter to it in *Walden*. Thoreau himself is musical. He plays the flute and sometimes sings as he walks outdoors. He says in another context that which is still applicable here: "Man's progress through nature should have an accompaniment of music. It relieves the scenery, which is seen through a subtler element, like a very clear morning air in autumn. Music wafts me through the clear, sultry valleys" (VII, 316).

Music not of Thoreau's own making draws his particular attention. The sound of Nathaniel Hawthorne's music box so enchants him that he walks to Hawthorne's house to hear it played. He eulogizes a music box's "exact measure" and feels that the assured beat signifies a loftiness in the strain ("the interjections of God") and that his hearing it must bespeak something in him as lofty (VII, 316–317). His response to a hand organ is equally pronounced but less reflective. Its delicious melodies, he says, tear him to pieces. It may be that, originating out of doors, this sound has increased its appeal for him. So it is with the town bells which he writes of in "Sounds," the fourth chapter of *Walden*. Their ringing is described as a "natural melody" (II, 136). By the time that it reaches his ear, it speaks for all nature since it has conversed with every leaf and blade of grass on the way. It is for this reason, apparently, that he prefers yet another bell, a tonking cowbell, which sounds in rhythm to the cow's essential movements in eating.

It has not been rung artificially and indeed has vibrated with the universal lyre.

The dominant sound described in Chapter IV of *Walden* is that of the locomotive. It seems "natural" in that its whistle sounds like the scream of a hawk. Yet the whistle's regularity — the farmers set their clocks by it — gives it away. The train is not natural, and Thoreau distrusts it. Its time is unlike the perfect time of the music box, the regular measure of which tells of "its harmony with itself" (VII, 316). The locomotive lacks this lofty harmony. Its sound does not come from God, and only its smoke *goes* to heaven — the cars are going to Boston. Thoreau therefore changes his image from that of a hawk to that of a horse, the usual iron horse in this case. The horse, we know, has been trained to harness in order to perform hard, routine work. Thoreau admires the purposefulness of his horse-locomotive, but he is ambivalent about the sounds it emits. Its "snort like thunder" and its "blowing off the superfluous energy" (II, 129, 130) seem heroic, while its "freight" of sounds — bleating of calves and hustling of oxen — give one the sensation of a pastoral valley going by. But he knows that this machine is whirling away the once prevalent pastoral life, and he does not want his ears spoiled by its hissing. Better to "thrust an avenging lance between the ribs of the bloated pest" (II, 214), he says later in *Walden*.

Alongside the railroad running past Walden Pond is the telegraph line. From this invention of man, Thoreau hears sounds with which he is in sympathy, for nature plays the tune. The wires humming in the wind are his aeolian harp. "Thus I make my own use of the telegraph," he says, "without consulting the directors" (VIII, 498). He listens directly to the humming of the wires, analyzing the sound, noting that the loudest volume occurs near a post, where the wires are tautest. Or he applies his ear to the post itself and hears the hum "within the entrails of the wood" (IX, 11). Then it seems as if every pore of the wood is seasoned with music. He compares the sound to that of an organ in a cathedral. As with sight, the auditory sensation is also something he can feel, but here he need not speak metaphorically. The ground at his feet does vibrate: the latent music of the earth, he says, has found vent in the telegraph harp.

This telegraph music has also induced a more rapid vibration of Thoreau's nerves, and he is both inspired and intoxicated. Indeed, these two terms with regard to his sensuousness are more or less synonymous. About thirty times in his *Journal* he must break out into a eulogy of this "most glorious music [he] ever heard" (IX, 219). In *A Week* he makes an implied comparison between it and the sound of the locomotive. The telegraph harp tells of things "worthy to hear, . . . not of the price of cotton and flour, but it hint[s] at the price of the world itself and of things which are priceless, of absolute truth and beauty" (I, 185). "Hint" is the key word here. To his imagination, such an enormous lyre, girdling the earth, must have divine blessing, for the winds of every latitude and longitude play upon it. He chooses to think that this is the medium for divine communication with mankind.

Thoreau is often intoxicated with purely natural sounds, such as bird songs. He makes special trips to various parts of Concord township to hear them, for example, the singing of warblers in Holden Swamp. But it is the strain of the wood thrush which prompts this outburst: "I would be drunk, drunk, drunk, dead drunk to this world for it forever" (XII, 39). It is, he says, a fountain of youth to all his senses and his favorite among bird songs. This accolade is noteworthy when we realize that the journal entries for most Aprils tend to be largely a record of his listening to the many spring birds. What sets the thrush's song apart for him, aside from its rich tone, are things which are applicable to his own lifestyle. The song is a product of one's total being (just as Thoreau would like his writings to be): it sings with all its "heart and life and soul" (XI, 254). Then too the bird sings, according to him, "for the love of the music," meditating its strain and "*amus[ing]*" itself with singing (X, 190). It has found an end in the means (as Thoreau has tried to do with his simple life). Also, the bird, he believes, preserves in its song the immortal wealth of the wilderness, mediates between barbarism and civilization (Thoreau wants the best of both worlds). The song is timeless and heroic; "it is unrepentant as Greece" (XI, 293). Two other favorite song birds of Thoreau belong to the thrush family as well. Like the wood thrush, the bluebird and robin are gentle birds with ethereal songs. He is pleased to have the bluebird's "soft warble melt in [his] ear" (XVIII, 5) and to hear the robin sing "continuously out of pure joy and melody of soul" (IX, 409).

As with his sense of sight, Thoreau in his hearing responds eagerly to "coarser" stimuli. A rooster's crowing, he thinks, is "the most remarkable of any bird's." He imagines hearing this bird in its wild state, its call "clear and shrill for miles over the resounding earth, drowning the feebler notes of other birds, — think of it!" (II, 141). The cawing of a crow to him is "delicious" (XIII, 112), while the calling of a loon is so thrilling that he could lie awake for hours listening to it when camping in the Maine Woods. He thinks that the call of this loon is superior to one heard back in Concord because here the call's wildness is enhanced by the surrounding scenery.

How Thoreau's other senses are fed, we see, affects his auditory response, for he is not only hearing the bird's voice but sensing the "voice" of nature as well. Thus when he hears the doleful notes of owls in his own native Concord, he thinks the sound "admirably suited to swamps and twilight woods" (II, 139), for it expresses the meaning of nature then and there. He loves to hear their wailing. Nature itself is but a musical instrument, and the birds and other creatures only touch the stops. Its sounds are the language spoken without metaphor (II, 123), a language which speaks directly to his sense of hearing. The sounds are pleasing in themselves, but because of their involvement with the whole of nature, they also have pleasing associations. A nuthatch's nasal call becomes "the handle by which [his] thoughts [take] firmly hold on spring" (XVIII, 15), for instance.

Other pleasing sounds to Thoreau come from animals other than birds and even from inanimate nature. He is refreshed by the barking of a dog at night (he likes to bathe his being in those waves of sound), and by the trump of bullfrogs, which he celebrates in *Walden* (only here it is the frogs amidst their Stygian chorus who appear to be the ones intoxicated). Insects too come in for their round of praise. A mosquito's hum affects him like a trumpet; it speaks of the world's vigor and fertility. The creaking of crickets particularly pleases him since he refers to it continually. He describes it as the most earthy, the most eternal, "the very foundation of all sound" (VIII, 306) — reminding him once more that heaven is here on earth. "Before Christianity was, it is" (X, 109). The fall of a dead tree in the Maine woods fills him with awe: it is "like the shutting of a door in some distant entry of the . . . wilderness" (III, 115), and he speaks in a whisper thereafter. A similar sound, made by thunder, he terms "Nature's grandest voice" (XIV, 349), and another such sound, the "rut" or roar made by the sea before the wind changes, causes him to catch his breath for an instant. Even wind moaning through dry oak leaves in winter is like the sound of the sea to him, "suggesting how all the land is seacoast to the aerial ocean" (XVII, 384). All the earth is vibrant with music, and Thoreau has shown us indeed his "appetite for sound" (XVI, 227).

Thoreau holds that the sense of smell is the most reliable of the senses. And there are odors enough in nature to remind him of everything even if he had no other senses. In spring all nature is a bouquet held to his nose, in fall a spray of fragrant dried herbs. He smells what he calls the "general fragrance of the year" (XIII, 361) and is almost afraid that he will trace the fragrance to one plant. Occasionally when he perceives a singular scent which he cannot identify, he walks about smelling each likely plant in an effort to find the source of the fragrance, while at the same time not neglecting the aroma of "old acquaintances" (XV, 5) which grow rankly nearby. Such a process leads him to the giant hyssop while in Minnesota. In Concord the process does fail once, with regard to a sweet new fragrance from a flooded grassland, but his satisfaction in trying to trace it to the wild grape, the eupatorium, and even the fresh grass is worthwhile in itself.

Thoreau is always on the trail of some scent, as his frequent hikes to Wheeler Meadow attest, and remembering all these fragrances is a balm to his mind. The emphasis, though, in indulging his sense of smell, is medicinal or restorative only by way of the enjoyment he derives from the exercise, an enjoyment which never seems to cease, for it stems from the whole range of smells. Whether he detects "earthiness" (X, 40) or a "certain volatile and ethereal quality" (V, 295), he is refreshed and expanded, as he says with regard to the odors wafted from the freight train rattling by Walden Pond.

The scents that might be termed ethereal are those like the fragrance emitted by the wild apple blossom. Thoreau esteems this flower for its copious scent and notes that the resulting apples are "worth more to scent your handkerchief with than any perfume which they sell in the shops" (V, 295). He perceives that another fruit, the wild grape, perfumes a river for a mile of its length, and he takes home bunches to scent his room. But it is the more pungent odors of nature that most intoxicate him. ("Intoxicate" is one of Thoreau's favorite words when he is describing how natural phenomena affect his senses.) The fragrance of evergreen woods he finds "bracing" (III, 17), and making up his bed while camping in Maine, he spreads spruce boughs particularly thick about the shoulders the better to smell the scent. Another evergreen, a club moss, becomes his smelling bottle. He is constantly bruising plants to gratify his sense of smell: hickory buds for their spicy fragrance; sassafras for its odor of lemon; black-cherry leaves for their rummy scent; pennyroyal for its medicinal aroma. This last plant he stuffs into his pockets to scent him thoroughly.

Even the vile odor of skunk cabbage invigorates Thoreau: "It is a reminiscence of immortality borne on the gale" (VIII, 5). This belief, we find, is echoed in his eulogy to the dicksonia fern: "To my senses [it] has the most wild and primitive fragrance, quite unalloyed and untamable, such as no human institutions give out, — the early morning fragrance of the world, antediluvian, strength and hope imparting. They who scent it can never faint. It is ever a new and untried field where it grows, and only when we think original thoughts can we perceive it" (XVIII, 349–350). His response here is similar to what his ear tells him about the telegraph harp or what his eye says concerning the color red. All speak to the primal man, to his blood and nerves, because what they say antedates time. These sensations were already present when the world was a continuous morning and man was youthful and heroic. So, Thoreau believes, man can be again — in this case, if he smell the fern. His sense of smell will have proved "oracular" (X, 40), and the world will be new to him.

If Thoreau smells every plant that he picks, he also tastes every berry that he passes by. Taste for him may well be an inferior sense since he refers to it less frequently than to the other senses; nonetheless, his walking companion at times, Ellery Channing, still concludes that Thoreau has an edible religion. What Channing probably refers to is Thoreau's *devotion* to sampling through taste almost everything that grows, his *reverence* of this activity. When Thoreau is in the Maine woods, for example, he finds that the *stem* of a round-leaved orchis tastes like a cucumber. One gets the impression that he has already tasted the other parts of the plant as well. While there too he engages in digging up lily roots (which means a great deal of slow, grubbing work amidst hordes of mosquitoes) and reports that the roots raw taste like green corn. The white froth oozing from pitch pines, on the other hand, has no taste at all, he says. On another occasion he taps an oak in late October to see why this particular tree gets its autumn colors so late. He finds it full of sap and immediately tastes it: "It has a pleasantly astringent, acorn-like taste, this strong oak-wine" (V, 282).

But Channing's statement is true in another way. Tasting (and eating and drinking) to Thoreau is religious if rightly conducted. By distinguishing the true savor of food and not being grossly concerned with the metabolic needs of the body (certainly Thoreau's position as he samples nature's variety), he is "relate[d] . . . to Nature, ma[d]e . . . her guest and entitle[d] . . . to her regard and protection" (XI, 331). Nature takes on divinity, and eating becomes "a sacrament, a method of communion, and ecstatic exercise" (VII, 372). For this reason he can, as he says in *Walden*, be inspired through the palate. His edible religion transmutes what might ordinarily be sensuality into an inspiriting sensuousness. He writes in the *Journal*: "After I had been eating . . . simple, wholesome, ambrosial fruits on [a] hillside, I found my senses whetted, I was young again, and whether I stood or sat I was not the same creature" (X, 219).

Most of what Thoreau drinks and eats may be termed simple and wholesome and often ambrosial. For a drink, we discover in *Walden*, he prefers not a cup of coffee, which would dash the hopes of a morning, but rather water. Even of water that has not yet settled, the kind he is offered at John Field's shanty, he drinks a hearty draught, while "excluding the motes with a skillfully directed undercurrent" (II, 299). In *A Week* he tells of lying down flat in order to drink "pure, cold springlike water" from horses' hoofprints (I, 194). When he cannot fill his dipper there, he digs a shallow well, using sharp stones and his hands, and is pleased no doubt that birds come and drink of its pure waters too. Again, as with his other senses, natural associations enhance his sensuous response. A more ambrosial drink for him is offered him while in the Maine woods, a homemade "beer":

> It was as if we sucked at the very teats of Nature's pine-clad bosom in these parts, — the sap of all Millinocket botany commingled, — the topmost, most fantastic, and spiciest sprays of the primitive wood, and whatever invigorating and stringent gum or essence it afforded steeped and dissolved in it, — a lumberer's drink, which would

acclimate and naturalize a man at once, — which would make him see green, and, if he slept, dream that he heard the wind sough among the pines. (III, 30)

Here indeed is the tonic of wildness, spoken about in *Walden*.

With regard to food, Thoreau may be tempted to eat a wild animal (a woodchuck in *Walden*), but when he tries such tonic of wildness (some squirrels in *A Week*), he abandons it in disgust. He generally has a repugnance to the eating of meat because of what he calls its "uncleanness" (II, 237). Here it is not so much the actual taste he dislikes — when some strips of moose meat are wound on a stick and roasted over an open fire in the Maine woods, he pronounces the food "very good" (III, 317) — but the accompaniments of preparation, the skinning of the animal and cutting up of the meat. The soil and grease and gore are simply offensive to him. But there is another reason why he finds flesh distasteful. When he speaks of the "small red bodies" of the squirrels (I, 237) and of the "naked red carcass" of a moose (III, 128), he is sensing that these animals, stripped of their outward guise of fur, are fellow creatures to him. As the human race improves, he says in *Walden*, it will stop eating animals as surely as savage tribes in their improvement leave off cannibalism.

Thoreau's greatest taste, then, is for vegetable food. He can get his tonic of wildness by eating wild fruit, the food he writes most about. Although he finds chokecherries to be scarcely edible, he enjoys the acrid-sweet savor of acorns and tastes sand cherries "out of compliment to nature" (II, 126). The acidic flavor of cranberries he terms a sauce to life that no wealth can buy. It is "refreshing, cheering, encouraging" and sets one "on edge for this world's experiences" (X, 36). His favorite among the wild fruits seems to be the wild apple, to which he devotes a separate essay, "Wild Apples." It is an "ovation" (XIII, 526) to taste one. He prefers to eat it out of doors, for not only does its savor seem to be increased then but the other senses are fed too: "[It] must be eaten in the fields, when your system is all aglow with exercise, when the frosty weather nips your fingers, the wind rattles the bare boughs or rustles the few remaining leaves, and the jay is heard screaming around. . . . Some of these apples might be labeled, 'To be eaten in the wind'" (V, 312).

The wind to Thoreau is a velvet cushion he likes to lean against. His sense of touch, thermal or tactile sensations, can never be sated. If the frosty weather bites one cheek, he turns the other; when the sun shines upon him, he "bathes" (XI, 38) in its warm presence. He prefers the warmth coming directly from the sun and not by way of radiation from the earth since it is direct contact for which he wishes. At night he wades through lakes of cold air that collect in a low pasture as one might wade in a lake of water. Wading through real water, he finds it "delicious" to let "[his] legs drink [the] air" (XVI, 349). He responds joyously to the touch of water as well, complaining only that he cannot seem to get wet through as he wishes. To him bathing means sensuous luxury: "To feel the wind blow on your body, the water flow on you and lave you, is a rare physical enjoyment" (X, 207). The effect is heightened because he feels in touch with the rest of nature too: a muskrat uses the same "tub," and a leaping fish dimples the surface of his bath water.

Another satisfaction which stems from bathing is the sensation which must follow: Thoreau rejoices to be wet so that he might be dried. Thus when he comes to a river while out hiking, he walks through, is dried by the sun and wind on the other side, and continues on. He says he would like to take endwise the rivers in his walks. That way, apparently, he would prolong the sensation of being wet and his anticipation of becoming dry. "Pray what were rivers made for?" (X, 202) he asks with regard to bathing. But he does find another use which gratifies his sense of touch—boating. He describes the sensation in his *Journal*: "The waves seem to leap and roll like porpoises, . . . and I feel an agreeable sense that I am swiftly gliding over and through them. . . . It is pleasant, exhilarating, to feel the boat tossed up a little by them from time to time. Perhaps a wine-drinker would say it was like the effect of wine" (XIV, 317). In *A Week* he says that undulation is the most ideal motion—yet another phenomenon to become intoxicated about.

On land, the kinesthetic element of Thoreau's sense of touch is emphasized. Not only does he perceive a kind of muscular movement in the earth, but he seems to participate in it. When he describes the earth in March as a great leopard lying out at length, "drying her lichen and moss spotted skin in the sun" (XVIII, 97), he suggests his own sensuous ease with the returning warm days. He does in fact describe this "skin" as a fur rug spread to be reclined on. He could stroke this mossy sward, he says; "it is so fair" (XVIII, 97). There are other times when he *has* to stroke the sward, as it were, in order to find his way back to his hut at night. Then his feet feel the faint track he cannot see while his hands feel the pine trees. This activity he describes as "pleasant" (II, 187).

With regard to the vegetation covering the earth, Thoreau, in gratifying his sense of touch, actively seeks out sensuous experiences. His position now is somewhat different from being more or less passive when the wind blows at him or water washes over him. Direct contact means the constant handling of the plants he sees, smells, or tastes. He picks up acorns because they feel so glossy and plump. With wet and freezing fingers he feels amid the snow for the green radical leaves of the shepherd's purse. Or he writes his name in the hoary bloom covering thimbleberry shoots. Such bloom, he observes elsewhere, like our finest qualities can be preserved only with delicate handling.

Thoreau realizes that a sensuous approach to nature demands that all senses must ever perceive in a fresh manner. With regard to sight, he knows that the time of day and the season of the year in which he looks at a particular phenomenon affect his perception of it. By letting an interval pass before confronting again this same phenomenon, he perceives some slight change in it. He becomes intimately acquainted with it, discerns its uniqueness. Thus he examines some aspect of nature in fair weather and foul—or better yet, as he says in *The Maine Woods*, is there while the change in weather occurs. The terrestrial browns, he finds, become "*glowing*" (XVIII, 45) when it rains. He observes phenomena too under various conditions of light, noting the change in appearance. When he sees the grayish andromeda against the sun, for example, he discovers the shrub to be the "ripest, red imbrowned color" and makes this note in his *Journal*: "Let me look again at a different hour of the day, and see if it is really so" (IX, 431). The seasonal changes are more striking, and even though expected, can still be truly an eyeopener: he writes that Flint's Pond in winter, once it is covered with snow, is so wide and strange that he can think of nothing but Baffin's Bay.

A change in vantage point is another way of gaining a fresh perception. By elevating his view, Thoreau, in "Autumnal Tints," finds that the forest becomes a garden. When he notices that the Concord River appears dark looking upstream and silvery bright looking downstream, he writes another memorandum to himself: "*Mem*. Try this experiment again; *i.e.*, look not toward nor from the sun but athwart this line" (IX, 394-395). And at Walden he inverts his head and notices that the surface of the pond resembles the finest thread of gossamer.[4] Often his changes in perspective border on the infinitesimal. He says: "It is only necessary to behold thus the least fact or phenomenon, however familiar, from a point a hair's breadth aside from our habitual path or routine, to be overcome, enchanted by its beauty" (XIV, 44). By turning his head "slightly" (V, 262), he sees the foliage of a maple appear to be flurries of snow, stratified by a driving wind.

Thoreau may also look narrowly through his eyelashes to see the landscape as an Impressionist painter might, or he may look above the object in question and see, as he says, with the under part of his eye. With this latter technique a stubble field in the light of a setting winter sun appears brighter than usual. He thus gains a fresh impression with what he elsewhere calls a sauntering of the eye rather than with a looking directly at an object. Similarly, a reflection in the water presents him with a new picture since he seems to see from all those many points on the surface of the water from which objects are reflected. A certain oak, for instance, looks greenish-yellow standing before some woods. Its reflection, however, is black and is seen not against woods but a clear whitish sky. The water permits him to see the tree from below and at the same time alters the coloring. He tells us in another instance that he gains "myriad eyes" (VIII, 253), while the contrast of the actual scene with its "rhyme" (IX, 403) in the water enhances both scenes for him.

Echoes are to the ear what reflections are to the eye and assist the sense of hearing to perceive in a fresh manner as well. An echo presents Thoreau with a new sound since the original sound has been transcribed through "woodland lungs" (VIII, 81). Again he notes the contrast, this time between the original sound and the accompanying echoes. At a lake in the Maine woods he notices that the echoes of a loon's laugh one morning are actually louder than the bird's call. The bird, he discovers, happens to be in an opposite bay under a mountain, and the sounds reflect like light from a concave mirror. Thoreau's position makes him the focus. Other contrasts in sound leading to a new perception can be obtained deliberately. For example, he submerges his head under water and then raises it to hear again the same sounds of nature but as if for the first time. Sometimes, he gains a fresh impression when he is not listening for any sound at all but has it break into his thoughts. This method may be termed a sauntering of his *ear*. As with sight, a fuller perception of a phenomenon occurs when he is outdoors to hear it at different times of day, at different times of year. At night, sounds seem amplified, since winds are usually calm; and in winter, sounds become clear and bell-like, having "fewer impediments [in the landscape] to make them faint and ragged" (V, 166).

As with sight and sound, so it is with Thoreau's other senses in trying to perceive in a fresh manner; he smells plants before and after a rain and in various stages of growth; he tastes wild apples in autumn and in winter after they have been frozen; he gauges the sun's warmth on his back during a winter walk and during a summer stroll. Each contrast amounts to a new sensation. He is always experimenting with his reception of sense data and thereby gratifying more richly each of his five senses.

3 A Horse to Himself

"The whole duty of man," says Thoreau, "may be expressed in one line, —Make to yourself a perfect body" (VII, 147). A superb condition of the senses, or their good state of health, will provide the chief condiments to perception. His thoughts about perfecting one's body— that is, achieving for it a consummate sensuousness—is here considered in the relationship of sensuousness to health; then to wildness, which points to an instinctive—or in Thoreau's terms, a western—life dependent upon the senses.

In a healthy body, Thoreau notes, all the senses receive enjoyment and each pursues its own gratification. Only the healthiest man can be fully sensible of the world around him. He in fact has resigned himself to its law of gravity, has made his axis coincident with its axis, and so, revolving in sympathy, has attained that sphericity which Thoreau recognizes as good health. The man's sensuous awareness extends in all possible directions, and he "resound[s] in perfect harmony" (XI, 424). But while health whets the senses, the invigoration which issues from using them *keeps* the man healthy. Thoreau says that "whatever addresses [them], as the flavor of these berries, or the lowing of that cow . . . —each sight and sound and scent and flavor—intoxicates with a healthy intoxication" (X, 218). Good health, then, is self-perpetuating as the healthy man uses his five senses: "The well have no time to be sick" (XII, 226). When Thoreau also states that people should have "Nature feel their pulse" to see "if their sensuous existence is sound" (VII, 224), he is in effect equating health with the sensuous life in nature. A response to sound is a measure of soundness, he puns. Similarly, fogs can be "touchstones of health" (X, 198).

Being aware of Thoreau's notion of the close relationship of sensuousness and health, we can now see another facet to his statement in
the first volume of the *Journal* that morality is not healthy (VII, 316).
Morality, strictly speaking, is not a question of having keen senses and
using them extensively. Sensuousness, as defined in the "Preface," is
*a*moral. However, morality in the large sense of the word—that transcendent goodness which informs our total lifestyle—*is* healthy, in fact,
cannot be otherwise according to Thoreau. He puts the idea in terms of
physical sensations: "goodness is one, though appreciated in different
ways, or by different senses. In beauty we see it, in music we hear it, in
fragrance we scent it, in the palatable the pure palate tastes it, and in
rare health the whole body feels it" (VI, 198). This body has attained
that sphericity, mentioned earlier. A perfect body has been made.

Always it is necessary to keep the senses undefiled. By not indulging
in certain pleasures of the civilized world, Thoreau can more acutely
sense the natural world: he prefers the everyday sky to the opium-
eater's heaven. One's body, he says, is a crystal well to be kept clear so
that it can register or reflect the surroundings. In another image he
writes in the *Journal* that a sick man keeps a horse to travel but the well
man is "a horse to himself" (XVI, 7). Thoreau's emphasis on the "perfect body" means one that, although purified, has not lost its animal
vigor. He agrees with Mencius, whom he quotes in *Walden*, that
superior men carefully preserve this quality, and he admires it whether
he sees it in the lower jaw bone of a hog (II, 242) or in the weeds
which choke out a crop (X, 250–251). If man departs from this rude
vigor, he can no longer really assimilate nature's elements generally.
Thoreau, then, suggests that we walk not primly about on our tiptoes
in nature but "healthily expand to our full circumference [the notion
of sphericity again] on the soles of our feet" (*LJ*, 201). It is such free
and solid, Antaeus-like contact which gains health and strength for us.
We should proceed boldly, confident of nature's friendliness (XVI,
252), knowing that disease can only overtake us from behind, not encounter us (VII, 75).

Thoreau does not completely unify his thinking on how one is to
obtain this health, to make himself a perfect body, however. The lack
of unity in his view has its parallel, and probably its origin, in his
thoughts concerning whether man is separate from, or part of, nature
and what his relative importance is in either case, thoughts which will

be discussed in Chapter 8. A sick man may draw health from a separate, although related, nature but cannot hope for this aid if nature is but a second self. Thus in one position Thoreau often contends that a constant intercourse with nature will ensure health, for "all Nature is doing her best each moment to make us well. She exists for no other end" (XI, 395). Nature is the only "panacea" (XVIII, 350).

How nature can give this health, we see, can take different forms with Thoreau, although all depend, to some degree, on a sensuous immersion — to be well in any season requires being *well* in it (XI, 395). In one instance the mere sight of pine cones and needles in the frosty air invigorates his body, he says. The sensation produces a pleasurable feeling, and this no doubt can be health-inducing. He is somewhat more involved with nature when he opens his mouth to the wind and is sensible of imbibing health, as though he were incorporating some of nature's vigor into his own body.

But nature's contribution to health may also be through a kind of correspondence. By seeing the sun rise and set each day, Thoreau feels himself related to a universal fact and feels his body's health preserved. It is as if he had made an investment in a corporation which never fails, an investment whose interest is paid in health. The workings of such correspondence is made clearer in this passage describing his response to the sound of flowing water: "It affects my circulations. . . . What is it I hear but the pure water-falls within me, in the circulation of my blood. . . . The sound . . . turns all the machinery of my nature, makes me a flume, a sluice-way, to the springs of nature. Thus I am washed" (VIII, 300). His body is stimulated and purified by nature.

In contradiction to what has been already said, Thoreau often states as well that nature is sick to the sick; that is, one can find health in nature only if one is already healthy. It is health which is the great landscape painter (XVIII, 368). This position of his parallels his belief about "shooting beauty," described in "Autumnal Tints" and discussed in Chapter 2 — that when one perceives any sensation, the quality must be in the individual first.[1] In his essay, "A Winter Walk," he says that only those who are "part of the original frame of the universe" can remain outdoors when a cold wind drives away all contagion (V, 167). They have the bodily vigor to be able to appreciate this wintry "health"; they have also enough summer in their hearts to complement the opposing season and so fulfill his criterion of a "healthy man" (V, 168). The best the people driven indoors can do, Thoreau implies in another essay, is to keep by them a book of natural history to read as a sort of elixir. These sickly people, to whom nature is sick, are like the reformers whom he refers to in *Walden* and whom he fittingly describes with an image related to health: they are not healthy because they "have a pain in their bowels" and so see their private ail in the social world. The world, they believe, must have been "eating green apples" (II, 85–86).

No matter how nature is seen, how he himself may see it, Thoreau is still convinced of its absolute health.[2] To describe nature, he uses such phrases as "inextinguishable vitality" (XX, 268) and "eternal health" (XIV, 44) and in *Walden* describes Mother Nature as "ruddy and lusty" (II, 153). "Why, 'nature' is but another name for health," he says, "and the seasons are but different states of health" (XI, 395).[3] He believes in nature's abundant health in all things—animal, vegetable, or mineral—and he is guided in his thinking so by his five senses. There is "health" in the hum of insects and in the strong odor of a dead horse (II, 350). There is "assured health" in bronzed oak leaves in winter (XV, 171) and in the very greenness of grass in summer—one of the strongest evidences of this quality. There is "pristine vigor" in the flowing sand of a thawing cutbank (IX, 348) and purity in a sandy beach, despite the bones of many a shipwrecked sailor buried there. In noting that the flavor of a cranberry or the fragrance of a water lily is compounded from the bottom of a bog or lake, he reflects that nature has health enough to turn corruption into something of beauty.

Nature's health really is one with its wildness. Thoreau attacks the views of those scholars who "describe this world as healthy or diseased according to the state of their libraries" (VII, 462). It is the state of nature, its wildness, which is the measure of health, he maintains, and is the source of that health. A wild storm shows that nature has not lost its primal vigor yet. To be out at such a time is inspiriting: one's senses are alerted. Even when Thoreau must remain indoors, as in his final illness, a snowstorm raging outside seems to energize him, according to the report of his friend Theo Brown, who happened to visit him during a mid-January blizzard.

It is in such circumstances that Thoreau's statement about his relation to wildness would most apply: "We are so different we admire each other, we healthily attract one another" (XV, 45). But when he is healthy, it is his affinity with wild nature that stimulates his sensuous life. He writes: "I seem to see somewhat more of my own kith and kin in the lichens on the rocks than in any books. It does seem as if mine were a peculiarly wild nature, which so yearns toward all wildness" (VII, 296); and elsewhere in affirming his "long[ing] for wildness," he describes wildness in terms which appeal to the senses — a place where the wood thrush sings, the grass is beaded with dew, and the soil seems fertile with yet unknown sensations (XI, 293).

In his essay, "Walking," Thoreau refers to three kinds of wild nature, all of which are welcome: "Give me the ocean, the desert or the wilderness!" (V, 228). The ocean is most fully described in *Cape Cod*, where he recognizes the tiger heart beneath its placid surface, very much as Melville does in *Moby-Dick, 1851.*[4] The depths are "wilder than a Bengal jungle" (IV, 188), Thoreau says. The sea breaks ships into pieces "in its sandy or stony jaws," while it "toss[es] and tear[s] the rag of a man's body like the father of mad bulls" (IV, 125). Yet we have seen his delight in the ocean in a previous chapter, his love of bathing in it and his fascination with its sounds and varying colors. When in Boston, he prefers standing on its wharves and looking out to sea to any of its urban enticements. In this kind of landlessness resides the truth of man's well-being, indeed of his very genesis (an evolutionary fact to be discussed elsewhere), and so something to which man should have periodic recourse.

The second type of wild landscape, the desert, Thoreau knows only at second hand, although he has a taste of it in walking the sandy reaches of Cape Cod. In spite of the desert having harsh, drought-ravaged features, he notes that it has pure air to breathe, compensating for its lack of fertility. From his reading of Richard F. Burton's travels in the Middle East, he believes that deserts, as well as oceans, can provide a suitable environment for a sensuous life, for he quotes the traveler, with apparent agreement, that in such locales there is "a keen enjoyment in a mere animal existence" (V, 228). And from his own reading of the Bible, he is aware that the desert can be more than its physical attributes — in at least four separate statements he refers to John the

Baptist's sojourn there. Thoreau knows that the land of locusts and wild honey can be both a sanctuary from, and a proving ground for, the civilized world. The desert tests an individual, confronts him with his primal self, and strengthens his resolve.

The third type of locality welcomed by Thoreau — "wilderness" — is, from the context of the statement, a specific reference to forested areas. This kind of wild landscape is the one with which he is most familiar, because of his excursions to the Maine woods, and about which he writes most. It is a country, we know, which also has much to appeal to the senses. It has a "wild, damp, and shaggy look" (III, 168) — the pungent evergreens are "diminished to a fine fringe" (III, 89) about the edges of jewel-like lakes, while the surface of the ground is "everywhere spongy" (III, 168) to one's foot. Through the trees come the scream of jay and grunt of moose. This latter animal for him is the true denizen of the wilderness, representative of this locale, and fills a vacuum there of which he had not been aware until he senses the animal's presence.

Thoreau contrasts this country with his own Concord, where the woods have been "emasculated" (XIV, 220) of their nobler animals and where he would like to see some of the domestic ones reassert their "native rights" and demonstrate that they have not lost their "original wild habits and vigor." A cow doing so, breaking out of her pasture and swimming a river, would be once more a "buffalo crossing her Mississippi" (VIII, 19). "We would not always be soothing and taming nature, breaking the horse . . . ," he writes in *A Week*, "but sometimes ride the horse wild and chase the buffalo" (I, 55–56). The "wild horse" corresponds to the moose of the Maine woods, which he describes as "God's own horses" (III, 132). We should take such wildness as our underlying support and follow the lead of the domestic cow-become-buffalo in having this wildness invigorate our actions. Thoreau suggests that man too has a Mississippi to cross, a west country to explore, a wild region to turn to account, which, like the forest (and the desert and ocean), is both a "resource" (III, 172) and "inspiration" (III, 173).

The west is synonymous with the wild in Thoreauvian nomenclature. In a Biblical sense, we know that the west points to a return to Paradise since Adam and Eve were driven east out of the Garden,

while historically we see that the American West has had Edenic connotations from the time of the very first colonies on the Eastern
seacost. All development, all opportunity, had to lie to the west. The
fertile groves and plains were waiting for their Adam, someone to
hold dominion over them. But "to hold dominion," the pioneers found,
meant attacking the wild beast and chopping down the forests where
they lurked. The west could be a threatening world of disorder as well
as an Eden. To Thoreau, however, the west remains a primal home. It
is not a teeming chaos that needs to be subdued but a resource to be
preserved — and a resource to preserve man: "in Wildness is the preser-
vation of the World" (V, 224). One literally comes to one's (five)
senses there, just as animals in the wild must rely on them. Furthermore, Thoreau, like other Transcendentalists, generally sees no danger
in the lack of restraint posed by the wilderness because man is not in-
nately sinful, as Calvin had said, but rather possessed of a divine spark.
This divinity is akin to instinct in much of what Thoreau says about
the subject, and the instinctive life, we find, is typical of wildness.
Wilderness might well fan the spark, promote a reliance on the
(divinely) instinctive life, a life where one marches to music that has
become a part of one's unconscious being.[5]

Thoreau praises such a life, for he defines a wise man as one who
obeys his never-failing instincts.[6] He himself would like to strike his
spade into the earth with the same "careless freedom but accuracy as
the woodpecker his bill into a tree" (I, 54). There is, in fact, no real
lack of restraint in this life because, first of all, instincts are not mere
whims but may be "the mind of our ancestors subsided in us, the experience of the race" (VII, 487) and, most important, the instinctive,
unconscious life has its divine basis: "The unconsciousness of man is
the consciousness of God" (I, 351). In the light of Thoreau's other
analogies touching on west and wildness, we see that it is God which
supreme wildness must represent. We do find Him described accord-
ingly in the *Journal*: in seeing a relation between the terms "willed"
and "wild," Thoreau writes that "the fates are wild for they *will*; and
the Almighty is wild above all, as fate is" (X, 482).

Some of Thoreau's other comments can now be fitted into this general
picture. He treats a swamp — which to him is the wildest retreat in
nature — in holy terms. It is a sacred place, "a *sanctum sanctorum*" (V, 228).

He writes of drowned sailors in *Cape Cod* as being cast ashore farther west, that is, as having come to God's realm. The western wilds are the place where one can find and experience God, just as another wilderness, the desert, was for the early prophets. When he himself "heads west" (an American colloquial expression for dying), he appropriately utters two words which epitomize wildness—"moose" and "Indian." "Will you not make me a partner at last?" he had asked earlier of God; "Did [God's scheme on earth] need there should be conscious material?" (VII, 327). The questions need no longer be asked, for he has finally achieved ultimate unconsciousness, wildness, west-ness.

Thoreau's concern while on this earth is to achieve a practical balance between living an instinctive life and a conscious life. He may state that he would rather be a dog and bay the moon at night than be an articulate Roman or that he would crow like a rooster in the morning without thinking of the evening. Thus could he express nature's *sound* state. However, he realizes that an animal's "knowledge," as John Burroughs says, consists in knowing but not in knowing that it knows. Its instinctive life, although thoroughly dependent on an extensive use of the senses, deprives it of an awareness of such use. Thoreau on occasion is "easily contented with a slight and almost animal happiness" (*C*, 222).[7] But in the course of time he cannot be satisfied with the instinctive life alone. If he wants to use his senses as a wild animal does, he also wants the fullest consciousness of such use. When he wants to give himself wholly to wild nature, he also wants to be wholly conscious that he is part of it. He will not in the long run emphasize one kind of life, unconscious or conscious, to the detriment of the other. "Both," he says, ". . . are good. Neither is good exclusively, for both have the same source. The wisely conscious life springs out of an unconscious suggestion" (XV, 37).

In "Higher Laws," a central chapter of *Walden*, Thoreau tries by a series of arguments to achieve a balance between the two polarities. He reverences, he tells us, both his inclination towards a higher life and his instinct towards a rank and savage one. He is tempted to devour a woodchuck raw, yet also feels a repugnance to animal food. Much of the chapter is about foods and eating, for this kind of appetite is one of the animal sensualities about which he feels he can write freely without offending anybody, including himself. He is using it as a representative of all animal appetites. In this chapter he proposes to bring, as E. J. Rose says, "the unconsciousness of animal life and the consciousness of spiritual life together without one weakening the other."[8] Thoreau can do so if he "transmute[s]" (II, 243) the energies arising from his animal nature into a spiritual use. As in "The Bean-Field" chapter, where he wants to make the earth say beans instead of grass, he here also wants to make use of earthiness (wildness) and make it say purity instead of gross sensuality.

"Higher Laws," then, is not a rejection of one's wild nature. Thoreau needs to maintain his Antaeus-like touch of the earth, we have already noted, and in this context it is to invigorate his conscious life. The chapter closes with an anecdote about a fictitious, but an appropriately named, John Farmer. *He*, being a laborer, needs to "recreate his intellectual man" (II, 245). Thus (the) Farmer hears someone playing a flute (Thoreau plays a flute) and a voice suggesting that he improve his life. All that he can think of is "to let his mind descend into his body and redeem it" (II, 246). Doing so would achieve the necessary balance for him. However, for Thoreau himself the process works both ways. It also makes *sense* (Thoreau would approve the pun) to have the body ascend into the mind and redeem *it*.

Another illustration of Thoreau's twofold position occurs in the description of his chasing a fox (VII, 186–187). Assuming that he has recorded the incident accurately, we see that at the start of the episode he is the conscious observer, his separation from the animal world emphasized by the physical distance—here, sixty rods—between the fox and himself. Then yielding to the "instinct" of the chase, Thoreau tosses his head aloft and bounds in pursuit as some predator would, snuffing the air as he does so. But while giving chase, he, unlike a wild animal, retains his consciousness and admires the graceful movements of the fox. When the fox doubles his speed, Thoreau once more "bound[s] with fresh vigor," wheeling and cutting him off. Having thus narrowed the space between them, both in physical distance and in kinship, Thoreau stops and observes the fox's movement again: "he ran as though there was not a bone in his back." Thoreau tries to be part of both worlds by alternating between them.

A more dramatic example of Thoreau's consciousness confronting wild nature occurs when he interrupts his stay at Walden Pond in order to journey to the Maine woods and climb Mount Katahdin. He becomes hesitant about wishing to be part of this world: he is *too* conscious of his separation from it. At the start of his climb, he finds the scenery exhilarating and at times is "scrambling" (III, 67) on all fours. The verb suggests his eager excitement, and the activity would not be unpleasant for a sensuous man who, we know, can hug the earth for joy. As the ascent continues, he becomes increasingly aware that this landscape is alien to him; it is not the gentle New England countryside with which he often wishes to merge. This fact is brought out by his use of a pastoral image in describing the rocks. They are herds of sheep or cattle, "chewing a rocky cud at sunset." So far the image is merely striking, but the next sentence suggests the hostility he feels directed towards him: "They looked at me with hard gray eyes, without a bleat or low" (III, 68). Similarly, the ranks of clouds are described as "hostile" (III, 70). He feels this country to be "vast, Titanic, and such as man never inhabits" (III, 70–71).

It is the *tonic* of nature Thoreau wants—here he receives a full dose. The "vast, Titanic" forces of Katahdin are pitted against his "(a)lone" self—both descriptions of protagonist and antagonist are repeated—and he is disconcerted, overwhelmed. To be part of this kind of nature might mean the irrecoverable loss of his knowing consciousness, and he will not brook such loss. He rejects the ultimate involvement with wildness here. In writing that "my body, this matter to which I am bound, has become so strange to me" (III, 78), he becomes aware that his unconscious being, his sensuous body, is a stranger to his knowing consciousness. His very self is being threatened, and the Katahdin episode ends with a cry of dismay, of alienation, of bewilderment: "What is this Titan that has possession of me? Talk of Mysteries! Think of our life in nature,—daily to be shown matter, to come in contact with it,—rocks, trees, wind on our cheeks! the *solid* earth, the *actual* world! the *common sense*! *Contact*! *Contact*! *Who* are we? *where* are we?" (III, 79) [Thoreau's italics].

It is remarkable that Thoreau's Katahdin experience seems to have had little effect on his subsequent thinking and writing. Even in the account of this excursion we find, a few pages further on, a reference to primeval nature as being blissful and innocent. What helps to prevent this incident from becoming a serious trauma for him is probably his *usual* sense of doubleness, his ability to stand apart from himself and observe that self, often with a bemused smile.[9] Such is his stance in many pages of *Walden* — when the Hermit-Thoreau laughs gently at his own mystical experience, for instance[10] — and even in the description of the fox chase where we see him humorously aware of the somewhat laughable figure he makes when he tells us of his "spurning the world and the Humane Society at each bound" (VII, 186).

In a later excursion to the Maine woods, Thoreau may be seeing himself in his earlier experience there when he says: "Generally speaking, a howling wilderness does not howl: it is the imagination of the traveler that does the howling" (III, 242). A decade after his climb of Mount Katahdin, he expands upon this notion in his *Journal*. He has just discovered a new kind of huckleberry in his native Concord, a small hispid berry which, when he tastes it, leaves a tough, hairy skin in the mouth. He feels he must be in Rupert's Land, the country which is his idea of wildness. He has recognized the land by the taste of the berry — although he says he could do "as much by one sense as another." What need, then, he continues, to visit far-off mountains? "It is vain to dream of a wildness distant from ourselves. There is none such. It is the bog in our brain and bowels, the primitive vigor of Nature in us, that inspires that dream. I shall never find in the wilds of Labrador any greater wildness than in some recess in Concord, *i.e.* than I import into it" (XV, 43).

Then when Thoreau returns from his original journey to the Maine woods to resume his life at Walden, he can say in the book that celebrates that life that "we must be refreshed by the sight of [nature's] inexhaustible vigor, vast and titanic features" (II, 350). While he seemed to have been shaken by those same "vast and titanic" features of Mount Katahdin (the identical adjectives are used in his description of the climb), he nonetheless insists here on what he believes should be our course. We need to respond to nature's wildness or to have the bog within us stirred up (the two actions really come to the same thing) in order to energize our lives. It is his wish that we not lose sensuous contact with the primal world, even if it be but in the taste of an inedible huckleberry. We also require, he says in the same paragraph from *Walden*, "that all things be mysterious and unexplorable" (II, 350). The exclamation, "Talk of mysteries!" from the bewildered cry in his Maine woods essay had stated what *is*; *Walden*, though, states what *should be*. Ever the loon of "Brute Neighbors," which represents the mystery, should elude him (II, 259–262). (The bird, we now know, is among the most primitive on the evolutionary scale and so epitomizes wildness.) Yet Thoreau will persist in his pursuit of the creature—just as before he had bounded after the fox—with no real intent of catching it, of permanently becoming one with it.

In his writings Thoreau refers to several objects in nature to symbolize his "border life" (V, 242) between the instinctive and conscious worlds. A pine tree standing on the verge of some clearing—its boughs pointing westward, its appearance weather-beaten, its presence near the cawing crow—might well be, as he suggests in the *Journal*, the emblem of his life. The bird seems to represent the purely instinctive world, while the tree is a kind of link to that wild world. He hears the crow's loud cawing echoing through a pine wood and thinks, "How wild!" (XII, 288). He blesses God for such wildness—"for crows that will not alight within gunshot!" (XIII, 113) he says in another instance.

Hawks too are associated with the pine tree, for Thoreau says outright: "The hen-hawk and the pine are friends" (XVII, 450). The hawk alights "almost within gunshot, on the top of a tall white pine" (XI, 236), but before Thoreau can bring his glasses fairly upon it, it is circling away again. It remains, like Moby Dick, an ungraspable phantom of life, and yet the sponsor of spermatic thoughts. He links its wild freedom with man's poetic or creative genius. "Flights of imagination, Coleridgean thoughts," (IX, 144) he speaks of its soaring course, with reference to Coleridge's distinction between fancy and imagination. The hawk's flight "tak[es] in a new segment, annex[es] new territories!" (IX, 143). Its circling flight is not a mere series of fanciful repetitions but a creative act. The flight is infinitely expanding, and Thoreau's conscious self is seeking to discover his relationship to this infinity.

Thoreau himself as a poet, a man of imagination, is also a "friend" (III, 135) of the pine, but, unlike the hawk, is so related to it because he consciously understands the tree's truest use. A sight of the pine branches swaying in the wind gives him to know that the living presence of the tree is more important than the produce it yields as timber. Thus he remains on the other side of the tree from the hawk.

The pine with which he has identified himself has to be one growing on the edge of, and not within, the wilderness (of unconsciousness). It is a *background* of wildness that feeds his poetic imagination, just as physical wilderness provides the raw material for civilization. Wildness is good, "not only for strength, but for beauty" (III, 173). And, he tells us in *The Maine Woods*, he prefers the clearing's edge to wilderness as a permanent residence. A wild wood skirting a town and sometimes jutting into it is inspiriting.

Thoreau's border position is seen also in his references to the bean field in *Walden* and to the apple tree in "Wild Apples." By hoeing beans barefoot, he is attached to the earth and gains strength from it as did Antaeus. But he has an implicit conscious reason for raising them apart from their practical value, that reason being "for the sake of tropes and expression" (II, 179). As a trope, the bean field represents the balance between the wild and the conscious which he is trying to depict. His bean field, he tells us, is "the connecting link between wild and cultivated fields" (II, 174). That he would identify himself with such a field is evident when he says elsewhere that he "would not have every man nor every part of a man cultivated, any more than [he] would have every acre of earth cultivated" (V, 238). Then he can eulogize the American wild apple, which was once an orchard plant. It has come to the same position as has the pine growing at the edge of a clearing—but from the other direction. The pine really is emblematic of mankind's evolution, the evolution of the race, while the apple tree is the truer emblem of the individual Thoreau. His comparison is apt when he says that "*our* wild apple is wild only like himself, perchance, who belong not to the aboriginal race here, but have strayed into the woods from the cultivated stock" (V, 301).

A primitive life, such as lived by the Indian, is man's closest approach to wildness. But while Thoreau states that "the Indian does well to continue Indian" (I, 56), he seems to be saying so on his own behalf rather than the Indian's. The Indian is nature's "inhabitant and not her guest" (VII, 253) and so holds a place between the civilized world and nature, something Thoreau can observe. He employs one as a guide on his Maine woods excursions "mainly that [he, Thoreau] might have an opportunity to study his ways" (III, 105). For to Thoreau the Indian can be another kind of link to wildness, as was the pine tree. Indeed, Thoreau compares the tree to him: "The pine stands in the woods like an Indian, — untamed" (VII, 258). He remarks about this "untamed" quality when he discusses how the Indian finds his way in the wilderness "very much as an animal does." The red man, Thoreau believes, relies on sources of sensuous information so various that he "does not give a distinct, conscious attention to any one." "He does not carry things in his head," Thoreau says, "but relies on himself at the moment" (III, 205).

The "untamed" way of life is not wholly acceptable as a model, however; only parts of it are. Thoreau recognizes that "the history of the white man is a history of improvement, that of the red man a history of fixed habits of stagnation" (XVI, 252). Furthermore, while in the Maine woods, as "chaplain" on a moose hunt, he reflects what coarse and imperfect use Indians as hunters make of nature. At their camp he sees where refuse pieces of moose meat lie about on the ground and other portions are cooked by being half buried in ashes, "as black and dirty as an old shoe" (III, 149) — and he feels called upon for sleeping to spread his blankets over the hides in camp, "so as not to touch them anywhere" (III, 150). Still, he wants to stand as "near to the primitive man of America . . . as any of its discoverers ever did" (III, 151), and his distaste in one excursion does not prevent him from visiting the Maine woods again in the company of another Indian guide, Joe Polis. Thoreau praises this Indian for "availing himself cunningly of the advantages of civilization, without losing any of his woodcraft" (III, 222). He is the kind of savage who can be described as getting iron arrow points and hatchets from cities "to point his savageness with" (III, 121).

In a similar fashion but in the reverse direction, Thoreau wants recourse to the wilderness. But he does not use the wild, the primitive, as merely a once-and-for-all starting point for another kind of life — hence his repeated walks to the wilder places of his native Concord and his many excursions to the ocean and to the Maine woods. Wildness is a state which must be often recalled, re-sensed, relived. It is his stronghold from which he never ventures far. He sees in the primitive life an emphasis upon healthy physical senses, which he favors, but equally important he sees in civilized life an opportunity for refining their use. Joe Polis — like the pine and apple tree, the bean field, and the gentle

New England countryside—epitomizes for him the desired balance between living an instinctive, western life and a conscious, civilized one. Thoreau really wants the best of both worlds—of the primitive and of the civilized world—a wish which we shall see is also true of his economic position.

4 A Taste of Huckleberries

Simplicity is central to Thoreau's economic position. In the *Walden* chapter which tells what he lives for, he not only cries out, "Simplicity, simplicity, simplicity!" (II, 101) in an effort to convince us that our affairs should be as two or three, but also changes his exclamation to a direct command a few sentences later: "Simplify, simplify" (II, 102). He "love[s] to see anything that implies a simple mode of life and greater nearness to the earth" (XX, 88), he says elsewhere. What he wants is an intimate or sensuous acquaintance with the earth and with the materials it yields when he secures, as simply as possible, his basic needs of shelter, food, clothing, and fuel. Indeed, his ideas about simplicity, as they apply to matters of economy, are largely derived from his sensuous impulses.

In the "Conclusion" of *Walden*, Thoreau comes back to an exhortatory stance after having provided us with the example of his own simple life in the preceding chapters. "Cultivate poverty like a garden herb" he tells us (II, 361). The image is aptly chosen. The "poverty" he speaks of is not a destitution that one falls into because of mismanagement of funds but a kind of life deliberately chosen and carefully nurtured. It yields satisfactions which grow out of the personal attentions required in pursuing a down-to-earth activity. This is the kind of "poverty," he says, "that enjoys true wealth" (II, 218), and engaging in such life himself, he finds fulfillment in his own "voluntary" poverty (II, 16).

A life of gratifying one's senses in nature is simple and inexpensive, and Thoreau seems to be an economic success by his own definition.

But he points out that there are two kinds of simplicity, that followed by the savage and that which the civilized man is capable of following. The savage's simplicity may be but a mere existence, his living simple inwardly as well as outwardly. The civilized man can adopt this outward simplicity not merely to live but to live as fully (or as sensuously) as possible. A primitive economy is a way of life close to nature; it tends to foster a sensuous enjoyment of the world; it clears away inessentials. From its vantage one may better see when the conveniences of civilization subtract more from life than they add. Thoreau is all too willing that we make use of some conveniences: "If we live in the Nineteenth Century, why should we not enjoy the advantages which the Nineteenth Century has to offer?" (X, 324). But in accepting only those "advantages" of civilization which contribute to a fuller life, a civilized man can well be the "wiser savage" (II, 44) of which he speaks.

In his simple life at Walden, Thoreau is the wise savage. He knows that a parlor is preferable to a cave if for no other reason than that it is cheaper and easier to build a parlor than to find a suitable cave in his neighborhood. The truly civilized man must solve the problems of life practically, not only theoretically—"if one designs to construct a dwelling house, it behooves him to exercise a little Yankee shrewdness" (II, 31)—and Thoreau's practicality works hand in hand with his sensuousness. Thus he builds his hut not of logs but of boards which he buys cheaply from an Irish laborer, having first to dismantle the man's shanty for them at six o'clock in the morning and then haul them away. The activity gives him opportunity to hear an early thrush, an experience which he finds worth recording. Other materials include "refuse" shingles, "secondhand" windows, and "old" bricks (II, 54)—all practical to obtain. He buys the lime, a comparatively expensive item, for making his plaster, but reports that he had made a small quantity of lime previously by burning the shells of river clams. Having done so gives him a personal association with the material, an important feature to him.

Apart from these initial expenses, the cost of the hut is little, for the cost of anything, says Thoreau, "is the amount of what I will call life which is required to be exchanged for it immediately or in the long run" (II, 34). His sensuous enjoyment in building his home close to nature is not exchanging life but living it. He speaks of the pleasant hillside where he works, with its view of the pond through the pine woods. He takes satisfaction in carefully mortising and tenoning the arrowy pines he has chopped down and is glad to sit amid the green boughs to eat his lunch, glad of the fragrance they impart to his food. But he stops not only for lunch. He pauses for more than a quarter of an hour to watch a torpid snake in the water; he takes note of the song of lark and pewee and hears a stray goose cackling over the pond. When he digs his cellar, he takes "particular pleasure" (II, 49) in breaking the ground, reflecting that he is but enlarging a woodchuck's burrow and that his house is a kind of porch at the entrance. The stones for the chimney he carries to the site by hand and so knows the heft of each. But he delays the building of it until the next fall and even then "linger[s]" about the work, "pleased" to see the *gradual* progress (II, 266–267) as he savors his task. The plastering is done in fall too, and he secures the clean, white sand for this purpose from across the pond with his boat, an experience "which would have tempted [him] to go much farther if necessary" (II, 271). He makes "no haste in [his] work, but rather ma[kes] the most of it" (II, 47).

The best workshop, Thoreau says elsewhere, is an outdoor one: it has the best scenery and acoustics. If he prefers keeping bachelor's hall in hell to boarding in heaven, he prefers keeping bachelor's hall in nature most of all. His hut will be a "solitary dwelling" (II, 79). Before moving to Walden Pond, he had written a review of the utopian booklet, *The Paradise within the Reach of All Men*, 1842, by J. A. Etzler. Etzler's utopia, based on collective action, had recommended the use of apartment houses. Etzler's notion — and those of the Brook Farm commune, the "heaven" at which Thoreau was asked to board — prompt Thoreau to defend his type of dwelling in *Walden*. He feels it is cheaper to build a complete little house than to find a suitable neighbor to share a larger one. He is generally distrustful of community attempts to solve life's problems, believing that solution must begin instead with the individual. Furthermore, there is the personal satisfaction of building his own house by himself — then he can live in it "as snug as a meadow mouse" does (II, 291–292) in a nest of *its* construction — and he also has his "horizon bounded by woods all to [him]self" (II, 144).

The interior of Thoreau's hut pleases his eye more before it is plastered than later. Rough brown boards full of knots are more satisfying to his visual sense than uniform gray plaster. But the fact that the structure consists of but a single room, he feels, is compensatory: "you can see all the treasures of the house at one view" (II, 269). His hut fulfills the requirements of the house he dreams of, being parlor, kitchen, and bedroom at once. Not only can you "wash, and eat, and converse, and sleep, without further journey" into other rooms (II, 269), but your senses immediately tell of things basic to human life. You can "pay your respects to the fire" directly (Thoreau maintains that the fireplace is the most important *place* in a house) and "hear" the pot boil that cooks your dinner (II, 269). Meanwhile, your eye can note the building's origin and purpose from its very structure.

Thoreau's ideas about housing have drawn praise from modern architects. Frank Lloyd Wright speaks of his wise observations on the subject. Wright, a proponent of organic style, believes that the form of a building should be a function of its site, its use, and the materials of which it is made. While Thoreau is not so much concerned with architectural aesthetics as with practical and sensuous considerations, his statements on the subject anticipate Wright's. For example, in *A Week* he commends the houses of the lockmen along the Merrimack River. The buildings are set high on a leafy bank, "with sometimes a graceful hopyard on one side, and some running vine over the windows" (I, 256). Since they blend with their surroundings, he says they are like beehives set outdoors. The impression they create can be compared to that made by muskrat houses, which he says in the *Journal*, are an "ornament to the river." He wonders if an architect could not take a hint from this conical shape: "Something of this form and color, like a large haycock in the meadow, would be in harmony with the scenery" (X, 422–423). In this relation he imagines that a boat turned upside down would make a good home for a sailor. Sometimes, if a building looks out of place in its environment, then the elements will naturalize it in time, he feels. Thus the unpainted houses of Cape Cod, with their high-pitched roofs, come to look comfortable and firmly planted as they grow weather-beaten.[1]

When Thoreau talks about a loggers' camp in the Maine woods, he is once more concerned about the structure's relation to the area and the appeal it makes to his sense of sight—the camp, he says, is "as completely in the woods as a fungus" (III, 21)—but most of his remarks have to do with the materials used in construction. In approving the fact that they come from those trees chopped down to make a clearing for the buildings, he seems to be agreeing with one of John Ruskin's premises on architecture, mentioned in *The Stones of Venice*, 1851–53, namely, that materials should be both near at hand and cheap. Thoreau, acquainted with Ruskin's earlier work, *Modern Painters*, 1843, and dismissing it as being concerned with nature only as seen by an artist, probably would also have found Ruskin's ideas on architecture too art-oriented,[2] although several of the British critic's notions parallel Thoreau's. Both men, for instance, argue against a division of labor in construction, believing that the designer and builder should be one, and Thoreau goes even further when he says that the dweller should be the designer and builder. But Thoreau arrives at his ideas independently, and they stem at least in part from the sensuous involvement which he desires. He wants to experience all the sensations accompanying construction, as we saw in his building of his hut. And when he refers to the materials of the "very proper forest houses" in the Maine woods, he emphasizes the appeal made to his sense of sight and also to touch and to smell: the houses are "made of living green logs, hanging with moss and lichen, and dripping with resin, fresh and moist, and redolent of swampy odors" (III, 21).

One architectural critic who might have influenced Thoreau was Emerson's friend, Horatio Greenough. Greenough was probably the first writer to apply organic theories to architecture, maintaining that the form of the building should grow out of its needs. Yet Thoreau in *Walden* refers to him as a "sentimental reformer" who "began at the cornice, not at the foundation" (II, 51). Thoreau, in fact, misunderstands Greenough's theories, believing that Greenough was merely taking existing architectural ornaments and trying to give them a core of truth (as one might stick an almond into a sugarplum, Thoreau says).[3] Thus when Thoreau states, in apparent disagreement with Greenough, that architectural beauty "has gradually grown from within outward, out of the necessities and character of the indweller" (II, 52), he is actually echoing the critic.

Thoreau, however, in his affinity for wildness, discussed in the preceding chapter, departs from Greenough in saying that this beauty should grow out of some *unconscious* truthfulness, a man having no more to do with the style of his house "than a tortoise with that of its shell" (II, 52). This is undoubtedly one of Thoreau's exaggerated statements — if not, how does one exercise the Yankee shrewdness he speaks of? — but we see that the thinking behind it prompts him to admire the Maine woods dwelling again. He comments on its naturalness as well as its further appeal to his sense of sight. It is "but a slight departure from the hollow tree, which the bear still inhabits, — being a hollow made with trees piled up, with a coating of bark like its original." No thought is given to ornamentation; yet the mosses, lichens, and fringes of bark "which nobody troubled himself about" make the "handsomest paint," and the projecting ends of the logs, sawed or chopped off irregularly, give the house a "very rich and picturesque look" (III, 138–139). It must be remembered that Thoreau here is not trying to be an explicit critic of architecture. He is voicing his emotional reaction to the subject. He wants to see "the honest and naked life here and there protruding" (XVI, 315), and he sees this quality most readily in the more primitive dwellings, where the shelter responds directly to the natural environment and relates the dweller to it.

During his Walden experience or "experiment" (II, 44), Thoreau wishes to give another aspect of a primitive economy a chance to prove itself. He at first thinks that he can live entirely to himself so far as food is concerned. He believes that he can easily raise his own rye and corn, grind them by hand, and so dispense with rice and pork. Sweets, he feels, he can make from pumpkins or beets or maple sap (II, 71). In so doing he will be close to nature and be receiving a sensuous enjoyment from his labor. The first year he plants two and a half acres, being obliged, however, to hire someone to do the plowing. Although he does hold the plow himself, and so maintains his contact with the primal earth in this basic operation, he feels more satisfied the second year when he spades up by hand all the land he requires. He reasons that then he is not tied to ox or horse and so can follow the bent of his genius.

That Thoreau's bent is a sensuous one is apparent in the description he gives of hoeing his rows of beans. Because he has no aid from domestic animals or hired help in this activity, he says he becomes "much more intimate with [his] beans than usual." But it is not only the beans themselves but also the sensations accompanying the work which are important to him. He feels the "dewy and crumbling sand" on his bare feet and notes its yellow color in contrast with the long green rows. At one end of the field is a shrub-oak copse, where he seeks coolness, and at the other end a blackberry plot, where he notices the fruit deepening its tints with each successive hoeing. Birds provide "sounds and sights [he] hear[s] and s[ees] anywhere in the row, a part of the inexhaustible entertainment which the country offers." When he refers to the imitative song of the brown thrasher, he anticipates the reader's query about what this has to do with growing beans by saying that the notes are a "sort of top dressing in which [he] ha[s] entire faith." Similarly, even the "music" of his hoe striking a stone yields an "instant and immeasurable crop" (II, 173–176).

When Thoreau describes, not the cultivation of food stuffs in the field, but their actual preparation for the table, the activity again appeals to his senses. Baking bread, for instance, is "no little amusement" as he tends and turns the loaves. He also wishes to retain their fragrance as long as possible "by wrapping them in cloths" (II, 68–69). It is no wonder that he can set aside questions about the intricacies of his diet by saying that he could live on board nails; his senses are already being fed.

When Thoreau interrupts his Walden experiment to travel to the Maine woods, he sees a potato field there which he feels is in keeping with his notions of a primitive economy. Trees have been felled and burned to clear a patch of ground, and the potatoes are planted amid the ash piles, the ash serving as fertilizer. The individual tending the field has retained a sensuous contact with the earth, experiencing all the rudimentary sensations of producing his own food — clearing, tilling, planting, and harvesting. The sensations are not diminished for him through the "help" of crew or machinery; nor does he lose the final sensation — that of consuming the fruit of his labor — through trade. Since Thoreau traveled to Maine for but three dollars, he observes that those in economic difficulty could go there too, plant a sufficient crop, and be as rich as they please, beginning life as Adam did (III, 15–16).

It can be argued today, of course, that Thoreau's views on primitive economy, whether concerning food or other basic wants, are just not applicable to our present world. There is just not enough individual farming land for our huge urban populations, and many of these people, moreover, have no aptitude for manual work. However, such argument is really beside the point. Thoreau is no more advocating that everyone return to the land than that everyone "adopt [his] mode of living" alone beside a pond (II, 78). As a sensuous man, he finds that the experience of direct contact with nature in supplying his basic needs is itself a necessity for maintaining his physical and spiritual well-being. He finds satisfaction in so doing, if only at intervals. What he advocates concerning economy is addressed mainly to those who are "discontented" and "complaining" of their lot (II, 17). He is simply telling them of a way to make their lives more meaningful, a way which has proved beneficial to him.

Thoreau himself, we find, once he is back at Walden, does not completely obtain all his necessities from nature; he does not completely avoid trade as he has once hoped to do. As early as his commencement exercises at university, he has contended that an antidote to commercialism could be found in an appreciation of the natural world; and in the first volume of the *Journal*, he has seen the farmer as the one keeping pace with the revolutions of the seasons while the merchant, to his disadvantage, only with the fluctuations of trade. Trade is artificial, Thoreau has said. Yet later he no longer gives unqualified praise to the life of the farmer, for he sees that this worker's gains can be "liable to all the suspicion which . . . the merchant's formerly excited" (XII, 108). Most farms have become just so many markets. And in spite of reaffirming in *Walden* that "trade curses everything it handles" (II, 77), Thoreau finds that he must be somewhat like the farmers he has come to criticize. He does sell beans and potatoes and buy molasses for sweets and also buys rice and pork. If he is monarch of all he surveys like Alexander Selkirk, the original for Robinson Crusoe, he also draws upon the effects of civilization just as Crusoe derived supplies from the shipwreck. He later concludes in his *Journal*:

> what is the use in trying to live simply, raising what you eat, making what you wear, building what you inhabit, burning what you cut or dig, when those to whom you are allied insanely want and will have a thousand other things which neither you nor they can raise and nobody else, perchance, will pay for? The fellow-man to whom you are yoked is a steer that is ever bolting right the other way. (XIV, 8)

Elsewhere he excuses his actions in this wise: "As for the complex ways of living, I love them not, however much I practice them" (XI, 446). He vows that he will get his feet down to earth wherever it is possible to do so.

A simple life based entirely on subsistence agriculture remains something Thoreau cannot seem to follow himself and something, we have seen, he cannot really advocate for others. Yet his Concord townsmen were curious about his "eccentric" life in the woods, and he most likely felt called upon to justify his experience in terms which business-minded people could understand. Much of his meticulous account of his economics in *Walden* was originally delivered as lectures to them. Therefore he appears somewhat as an archetypal middle-class shop-keeper, like Crusoe, and he is well aware that a comparison can be made, he being basically sympathetic with Crusoe's simple life. He is as ready to notch the nick of time on his stick and keep an account of his attempt to live in nature as was the shipwrecked sailor. Both men take a tradesman's pride in their workaday accomplishments: Crusoe tells us he "wanted nothing but [he] could have made"[4]; Thoreau tells us he has "as many trades as fingers" (II, 65). Thus their bookkeeping, about obtaining the basic necessities of life, proceeds.

It is a curious fact that both men enter into their experiences because they do *not* want to settle down to business in the usual sense of the term. But there some of the similarity ends. Crusoe directs his principal efforts in the first years of island life to trying to escape from his confinement and to return to the commercial world he knows. When he cannot do so, he applies its values to the resources at hand. The writing materials he salvages from the ship mean more to his book-keeping mentality than the dog which he also finds there. The money on board he decries as the root of all evil—yet upon second thoughts takes it along too. He is striving for worldly success, even where none may see it. Since he believes himself singled out by Providence for having survived at all, it is a short step for him to see religious significance in any of his enterprises and to identify the hard work necessary for success in them as a religious virtue.

Thoreau, on the other hand, has from the start deliberately chosen his course of action, wishing to drive life into a corner and discover what it is all about. His criticism is directed *against* his countrymen, whose work leaves them "no time to be anything but a machine" (II, 6). He reminds them that "money is not required to buy one necessary of the soul" (II, 362). He finds that he need work only six weeks a year in order to maintain himself and thus contradicts the Biblical statement that one should eat bread by the sweat of his brow. He measures his success not in the number of goods he can accumulate but in the number he can do without, advocating an annual "busk" to dispense with impedimenta. Whereas Crusoe sees nature only as something to be exploited in an economic sense (he is blind, especially color-blind, to nature's beauties, never noticing a tropical sunset nor the brilliant plumage of island birds), Thoreau has arranged his life so that he has ample time to accomplish the self-appointed tasks which he describes in "Economy": hearing what is in the wind, watching from some tree or cliff, and inspecting snowstorms — all sensuous activities. His account of his economic affairs is really something of his brag to a world holding mercantile values, if not also, with expenditures listed to the last half cent, something of a tongue-in-cheek rationalization of a life sought simply because he enjoyed it.

After his stay at Walden, Thoreau throughout his life does continue in a limited manner to practice a primitive economy even while making use of the conveniences of civilization. He will be removed as little as possible from a sensuous involvement in satisfying his bodily needs. Eight years after leaving the Pond, he still says: "I like best the bread which I have baked, the garment which I have made, the shelter which I have constructed, the fuel which I have gathered" (XIII, 503). Although his shelter is once more the family house in town, he had helped to build it, and his frequent camping excursions elsewhere allow him to erect repeatedly the tent he uses.

As for clothing, Thoreau typically buys his shoes but keeps them supple by rubbing them himself — not with prepared polish, but with homely tallow. And he comes to dress in unfashionable corduroy, for it wears exceedingly well. He knows that, during the life of the material, the sun, wind, and rain, which he enjoys experiencing, will have ample time to shape the garment to the needs and character of the wearer. He is distrustful of modish clothes produced by the factory system, for it tries, he believes, not to clad people honestly but to enrich the controlling corporation. Clothing to him is a minor concern anyway compared with the demands of his sensuous nature, "compared with being able to extract some exhilaration, some warmth even, out of cold and wet themselves" (XI, 497).

With regard to food, Thoreau continues his experiments, and so continues to indulge his five senses. He is always gathering his crop from woods and fields and waters, he tells us. He chews raw turnips, hoping to realize the life of livestock, "for [eating them] might be a useful habit in extremities" (VIII, 305). Later he boils a quart of acorns for breakfast but finds them bitter compared to raw ones. In having eaten them raw first, he seems to be emulating the young man he tells of who tried to survive on dried corn, using only his teeth as mortar. In remarking on the success of the squirrel tribe in this venture, he may also be hoping to realize these animals' lives. Other experiments by Thoreau include making syrup from yellow-birch sap, if only two teaspoonfuls from every two quarts of sap. He tries to make maple sugar, but the results seem equally unsuccessful. His father tells him that he, Henry, already knows how to make maple sugar for less than it now costs him, that the making of it takes him away from his studies. Henry Thoreau replies that making maple sugar is his study.

Another "study" for Thoreau is collecting firewood each year. He writes of this activity several times in his *Journal*, usually at length and always with enthusiasm. The reason why he responds in this manner is found in the following statement about the work: "The pleasure, the warmth, is not so much in *having* as in a true and simpler manner *getting* these necessities" (XIV, 31) [Thoreau's italics]. He is like the woodsman in Robert Frost's poem, "The Wood-Pile," who, having sawed a load of cordwood in a bush, leaves the pile to molder, the work apparently being sufficient satisfaction for him.[5]

For Thoreau, even though he *gets* little fuel as he cruises in his boat searching for driftwood, he can *get* beauty, which he says, is perhaps more valuable. The "price" of such a little wood may seem high, but it is the very thing which he delights to pay. He says he is already warmed by his labor, the most waterlogged wood which he hauls into his boat giving the most heat. This observation is obviously true physically because of the exertion he expends. But when he says that the greater the distance he conveys the wood the more he is warmed "in [his] thought" (XIV, 30), then his statement is chiefly true because of his sensuousness. His other comments bear out this interpretation: he speaks of a dazzling summer duck which he saw during the activity, the rustling tortoises in the sedge which he heard, and the glowing shoreline which he envisions again in his mind.

The following passage is typical in describing the difficulties Thoreau encounters in obtaining fuel and how these difficulties contribute to his sensuous pleasure:

> I enjoyed getting [a] large oak stump from Fair Haven some time ago, and bringing it home in my boat. I tipped it in with the prongs up, and they spread far over the sides of the boat. . . . It . . . sunk my boat considerably, and its prongs were so in my way that I could take but a short stroke with my paddle. I enjoyed every stroke of my paddle, every rod of my progress, which advanced me so easily nearer to my port. It was as good as to sit by the best oak fire. I still enjoy such a conveyance, such a victory, as much as boys do riding on a rail. (XIII, 504)

He is "warmed" once more by the wood after he gets it home and before he actually burns it. He derives a separate pleasure from every stick that he finds, observing its curiously winding grain as he handles it, and takes joy in anticipating how he might split it most easily. His attitude is represented now in another poem by Frost — "Two Tramps in Mud Time."[6] Thoreau, like the poet, has united his avocation and vocation at the chopping block.

Finally, when Thoreau comes to burn the wood, he remembers the circumstances under which he found it. The thought of all the wood he has salvaged does not bring on weariness — unlike Frost this time, who had become overtired with his harvest of fruit in "After Apple-Picking" and harbored second thoughts about human effort.[7] For Thoreau, each burning stick of wood has a history which he continues to cherish. He becomes "a connoisseur of wood at last" (XVI, 116), his sensuousness ensuring that each stick in turn will be among the best he has found. No one can enjoy his fire as much as he when he watches the darting flames, the "serpentine course" (III, 116) of the ascending sparks. When the fire is no longer open but shut up in a stove, he feels he has lost a dear companion. Yet from a distance he delights in any rising column of smoke. It is the subject of one of his better poems, "Smoke," which he includes in the "House-Warming" chapter of *Walden*, while his essay, "A Winter Walk," comments further on this phenomenon. It signifies to him a human foothold, a civilization, and the establishment of the arts (V, 174). The fuel that we have seen as capable of "warming" man in so many ways also frees man to employ his own animal heat not for mere survival but to direct it towards creative effort.

The best work for Thoreau becomes that in which the end is found in the means. Labor is its own recompense, industry its own wages. The laborer can be cheated of his earnings only if he does not earn them, that is, if he does not make his work his pastime as Thoreau himself does when, as he says, he *plays* with an axe about the stumps of his woodpile. If the laborer does not earn them, he is postponing life, hoping to buy it back later. He is like the broker, referred to by Thoreau, who hurries to Boston to deal in stocks, an employment he does not relish, in order to *get* a living. Why not live now? Thoreau wants "instant life" (XI, 444). Better to be the poor Irishman who scratches away at his potato field, not overly concerned with the future yield but letting "the day's work praise itself" (IX, 17).

Life once lost cannot be regained. Therefore Thoreau ever attacks the practice of division of labor since such work too is a postponement of life. He will have none of it, for it denies him a satisfactory use of the senses in the present moment: "After a hard day's work without a thought, turning my very brain into a mere tool, only in the quiet of the evening do I so far recover my senses as to hear the cricket, which in fact has been chirping all day" (VIII, 268). Yet, he realizes, most men are becoming tools of their tools (VII, 368), their lives hasty and trivial. He prefers to live fully as he goes along.

It is true that division of labor tends to produce an abundance of goods inexpensively and so contributes to the high standard of living which we have today. But Thoreau does not want an improved means which may lead only to an unimproved end after all. He recognizes that the abundance of goods may create artificial wants and that a life of gratifying them makes for an artificial life. "Superfluous wealth can buy superfluities only," he says (II, 362). A wealth of goods may in fact be impoverishing, for with them one but acquires an expensive habit of living in which "necessaries" cost more than formerly. This habit cannot be maintained, the artificial wants cannot be gratified, in hard times. Demands fluctuate, and the result, he suggests, is unemployment for those who toil in a division-of-labor economy.

Thoreau's chief criticism is directed at the quality of life which ensues from such economy. Even when employed, the worker can find no real joy in a menial, repetitive task. He experiences but one stage in the production of an article, an article which most likely has no direct relation to his basic needs of food, shelter, and clothing. He thus fails to front the essential facts of life in that manner which Thoreau believes to be satisfying. How barren this worker's life is compared to that of some Indian who, wishing to catch some fish for his meal, sits down on a riverbank and weaves a fish trap![8] Conceiving the finished wickerwork in his mind first, the fisherman gathers the raw materials — the osiers growing along the shore — and completes the entire product himself. His creation is something of beauty because it has meaning to him (XVI, 313–314). He knows the history of each pliant red withe woven into the basket as surely as Thoreau is acquainted with each stick of the firewood he burns. When the Indian does use the trap, it will be not only fish that he catches. He has already caught life itself while making the artifact.

Thoreau would like to eliminate all middlemen in the process of living. Living is too dear to lose any of it: "if I buy one necessary of life, I cheat myself to some extent, I deprive myself of the pleasure, the inexpressible joy, which is the unfailing reward of satisfying any want of our nature simply and truly" (XI, 445). Only those who pluck their own huckleberries, for example, can really taste them. The finest part of the fruit is something which cannot be bought; otherwise, going to market and going a-berrying would be synonymous expressions. Picking berries, however, means an afternoon out of doors and a gathering of "health and happiness and inspiration and a hundred other far finer and nobler fruits than berries" (XX, 56). In tracing the origin of the word "fruit" to the Latin *fructus*, which means that which is *enjoyed* or *used*, he reaffirms his notion that the value is not just in providing bodily nourishment or even in satisfying just the sense of taste. The other senses receive enjoyment too. Emerson, in his address at Thoreau's funeral, regretted that Thoreau had had no more ambition than to captain a huckleberry party. Thoreau would have no regrets. As he says, he served his apprenticeship in the huckleberry field and did considerable journey work there. Huckleberrying provided him with "some of the best schooling [he] got, and paid for itself" (XVIII, 299).

Thoreau's economy really amounts to obeying Emerson's dictum of saving on one level of life the better to spend on another. If he sits on a pumpkin rather than on a velvet cushion, it is that he can have the entire pumpkin to himself whereas he might be crowded on the cushion. He knows meanwhile that nature provides many stools other than pumpkins. Again, if he saves on India tea, he splurges on pennyroyal, arborvitae, cedar, spruce, checkerberry, snowberry, and hemlock tea. He also eats purslane and rock tripe without cost, enjoying nature's unlimited stock. "The fields and hills are a table constantly spread" (XI, 300); he need not be frugal in their use. Always he wants to live simply but to extract much from little. If he is not rich in money, he is rich in time and opportunity to feed his senses. He spends his days lavishly—musing by the side of a wall on a September afternoon, listening to a cricket's siren song and watching the slanting rays of sunlight gild the mulleins. He wants a broad margin to his life. He can think of nothing worse than being a slave driver of oneself.

Thoreau, then, admires the simple men of Concord—the farmers, fishermen, and muskrat hunters—who approach their tasks, "surrounded by a wide halo of ease and leisure" (VII, 356). They enjoy their basic labors. He sees fishermen at a river who pursue their calling not solely as a sport nor a means of subsistence but as a devotion—just as he collects firewood along the shore. The muskrat hunters return weather-beaten to their huts from a day's outing along a flooded river, but their activity has made them "perhaps the most inspired by this freshet of any." They have been hunters of more than rats, he feels, and adds—"so God loves to see his children thrive on the nutriment he has furnished them" (XVII, 423–424).

Of the farmers, old George Minott is one of Thoreau's favorites. He "does nothing with haste and drudgery, but as if he loved it," yet he "is not poor, for he does not want riches." Minott's life embodies all the salient features of Thoreau's economy: "He makes the most of his labor, and . . . . is paid by the constant satisfaction which his labor yields him. . . . If another linter is to be floored, . . . he goes slowly to the woods and, at his leisure, selects a pitch pine tree, cuts it, and hauls it or gets it hauled to the mill; and so he knows the history of his barn floor." The old farmer "handles and amuses himself with every ear of his corn crop as much as a child with its plaything, and so his small crop goes a long way" (IX, 41–42). He allows no hired man to rob him of the sensuous pleasure he takes in his work, and apparently still finds time to walk in a swamp to hear the wind in the pines. Like the artist of Kouroo, he does not need to "find" time but has more or less been liberated from it in pursuing his daily creative activities.

Like Thoreau himself, Minott has made the economics of living poetic, made it a thing of beauty. For Thoreau does say in *A Week* that his life has actually been a poem, the poem he "would have writ, / But [he] could not both live and utter it" (I, 365). He differs from farmer Minott in doing both, nonetheless. When he does utter it, his writing style, like his economy, will be seen to be both simple and extravagant.

5 Sauce to This World's Dish

Thoreau describes an author in these terms: "A writer, a man writing, is the scribe of all nature" (VIII, 441). Thoreau's definition here is akin to Emerson's notion of a scholar being "Man Thinking."[1] In each case the individual, "man writing" or "Man Thinking," is a man first — a complete man experiencing corn, grass, atmosphere, and other phenomena of nature but having a delegated task. For him, living is the total act; writing or thinking is but a partial act. Thus Thoreau finds that "it is not easy to write in a journal what interests [him] at any time, because to write it is not what interests [him]" (I, 354). Living, that is, being sensuously alive, is of the first importance.

This is a significant priority to bear in mind in a study of Thoreau's writing style. His style is concrete, reflecting direct experiences. This fact is further brought home to us by his own comments about writing; while reference to related styles of other writers and speakers which he admires — from those of seventeenth-century writers, particularly the metaphysical poets, to those of earlier men who wrote at the dawn of nations' histories, even back to those of primitive man himself — can help to enlarge our understanding of Thoreau's concrete style. Its features, some seemingly diverse — simplicity and elaboration, for example — are seen to be really linked as manifestations of his sensuous nature. The writing appeals to our senses in concise images and in accumulations of phrases. The images may be homely or sophisticated; the phrases en masse may reinforce each other to produce the desired sensation in our mind or may create rhythms that invite a kind of physical participation through minute sympathetic movements in the fiber of our being. Thoreau not only makes clear his own empathy with the phenomena described but secures ours as well.

Thoreau is ever determined not to become lost in abstractions, for he contends that what interests the reader is the intensity of the life excited. On those occasions when it seems he might soar in a philosophical manner, he soon comes down to earth with some illustration which makes us see, hear, taste, smell, or touch what he himself has felt or thought. A reference to the vicissitudes of man's life, for example, ends with a statement that the fluctuating stream of life may flood and drown all the muskrats.[2] Note the following passage in which an image of cranberries makes an abstract idea concrete:

> Every man, if he is wise, will stand on such bottom as will sustain him, and if one gravitates downward more strongly than another, he will not venture on those meads where the latter walks securely, but rather leave the cranberries which grow there unraked by himself. Perchance, some spring, a higher freshet will float them within his reach, though they may be watery and frost-bitten by that time. Such shriveled berries I have seen in many a poor man's garret, ay, in many a church-bin and state coffer, and with a little water and heat they swell again to their original size and fairness, and added sugar enough, stead mankind for sauce to this world's dish. (I, 413–414)

Here we have not just a one-to-one relationship in which cranberries stand for the valuable things in life. Such an equation, stated directly, takes the image out of its natural setting of meadows and freshets where we find the frosts of winter and the mildness of a spring day. Thoreau's image does have its import as metaphor, but it also gives us the feeling of sensuously partaking of his own outdoor experience.

Thoreau's writing style here verges on the elaborate, as it often does, although his bias, so far as his direct comments on the subject are concerned, usually tends toward simplicity. Thus he says in *A Week* that it is not the overflowing of life but rather its subsidence which should be the impetus for writing (I, 194). In line with this image is his reference, a few pages later, to the writer being a sugar maple whose significant yield, apparently, is not a syrupy solution but a more concentrated product. Yet we often see in Thoreau's prose—and not only in the *Journal*—the refining process taking place then and there. We get both syrup and sugar: as in most of his concerns, the means share importance with the end.

Typically, Thoreau has here compared the writer and his art to a living organism, for his aesthetic notions in this case are similar to those which relate to architecture, discussed in the previous chapter. The writer should "bear" his poem, he tells us, as naturally as an oak bears its acorn (I, 94). The artifact is something that grows out of, is integral with, the person's life. Like the tortoise mentioned in *Walden*, which has no conscious control of the architectural design of its shell, so the writer finds his "natural" creation to be "*un*accountably" beautiful (V, 231) [my italics]. Its worth is known not by a contrived felicitous expression or by any serious thought it suggests so much as by what Thoreau refers to in terms of sensuous appeal—the fragrant atmosphere surrounding it (*LJ*, 166–167). Elsewhere he says that this fragrance should exhale as necessarily as the odor of muskrat from the clothes of a trapper.

Nothing more is required by the writer of genius than a cultivation of life—in Thoreau's terms, a sensuous involvement with it—to produce an organic work, says Thoreau. The work may be rough-hewn but its value permeates the structure. It has an ingrained polish which cannot be dulled. A cultivation of art, on the other hand, can varnish and gild, he tells us, but it can do no more: "Not all the wit of a college can avail to make one harmonious line. It never *happens*" (VII, 151) [Thoreau's italics]. He in fact is arguing for artlessness, which he elsewhere describes as the highest condition of art. Such creation really amounts to the artist's life itself, what he becomes through his work, rather than the artifact.

Thoreau knows, however, that man, unlike the instinctive tortoise, manipulates his artist's materials consciously and does produce a separate artistic work. Thoreau is as skillful a craftsman with words as he is a tradesman in economic matters. His *Walden* undergoes seven revisions before it is published. What he can aim for as a conscious writer is to produce a "page with as true and inevitable and deep a meaning as a hillside, a book which Nature shall own as her own flower, her own leaves; with whose leaves her own shall rustle in sympathy imperishable and russet" (VIII, 5). Writing in a journal those events that he himself has just experienced, he feels, will achieve these qualities, and if he does revise the accounts for publication, they will still be allied to life.

Thoreau is like the metaphysical poets of the seventeenth century, whom he much admires. They all try to express a thought or feeling as something physical, to write of both in terms of sense impressions. Thoreau, we note, singles out George Herbert[3] as one of the few writers who show *affection* for God, and we see that Herbert does so by treating of this emotion in concrete terms—in the poem "Love (III)," God is pictured as a kindly innkeeper hospitably tending to the traveler's needs of food and rest. Herbert has domesticated religious passion, made it, as Thoreau would say, an event in the "history of the body" (IX, 36). In some other poems, Herbert has tried to make the very shape of the poem, as it appears on a page, a visual counterpart of the meaning. Examples are "The Altar" and "Easter-wings." Thoreau too makes a similar appeal to the eye with one of his better poems, "Sic Vita, " which begins with the lines—"I am a parcel of vain strivings tied / By a chance bond together" (I, 410–411). Each stanza is shaped like a spray of flowers tied about the stems. These lines in the restlessness they express, are reminiscent of another poem by Herbert—"The Pulley." But Thoreau's poem may be more akin to those of another metaphysical poet, John Donne, in the striking quality of its conceit. Thoreau writes of the *anatomy* of his mental condition—his ambitions bizarrely "dangling" this way and that, the physical process of their sustenance detailed in the words, "Drinking my juices up."

In his writings Thoreau quotes John Donne[4] several times, and seems to find in this metaphysical poet a sensuous delineation both of love of God or of love of woman which matches in intensity his own love of nature. Donne's notion that God should "ravish" him ("XIV" of "Holy Sonnets") has its parallel in Thoreau's idea that all nature be his bride, already referred to in a previous chapter. Donne's notion, too, that love can make a room "an every where" ("The good-morrow") has its parallel in Thoreau's love for his native Concord, which place becomes for him an epitome of the universe. But it is Donne's concrete style, his ability to make writing seem, in Thoreau's terms, "a product of our physical organs" (VII, 370), which chiefly fosters Thoreau's interest. Says Thoreau: "The body, the senses, must conspire with the mind. Expression is the act of the whole man" (VIII, 441). In a later journal entry he goes even further than Donne, whom he quotes: "The poet's words are, 'You would almost say the body thought!' I quite say it" (XIX, 70). "Thoughts which the body thought," as well as "facts which the mind perceived" (IX, 99), are what concern him.

Like the metaphysical poets, Thoreau tries to jar us into sensing the uniqueness of everyday occurrences that we have become dulled to, those parts which he would gladly relive or re-sense. "We cannot write well or truly but what we write with gusto" (VIII, 441), he says. It is vain to write on the seasons unless the seasons are in you; if they are not, the writing will contain lifeless words, words that have a "paralysis in their tails" (X, 225). He wants those vascular and alive words that Emerson says form the language of everyday activities. It is for this reason that Thoreau prefers primitive speech to "white man's poetry" (I, 56). Several paragraphs of *The Maine Woods* are given to a discussion of the native language of his Indian guides. They "nail" a word to its original sense (V, 232). Thus the Indians distinguish by particular name those bodies of rough water which mean exhausted paddling for them from those of smooth water which indicate a rest for weary arms. Their words for other things tend also to be concrete and based on their own experience, the Indians apparently having difficulty in conveying an abstract idea. Thoreau especially likes the names which designate their months of the year because these names appeal to the senses. February, for example, is the moon of hard-crusted snow (one can imagine the crunching sound on a clear night), while March is the moon of sore eyes (here one can envision the glare from melting snow).

A use of language which comes very close to the Indian's, Thoreau feels, is that of the fur trader Alexander Henry. His travel account of the Canadian wilds stems from "an intimate experience, and he does not defer too much to literature" (I, 231). His journey and his ensuing report were integral with his workaday life. Thoreau praises the account for its "naturalness" and "directness," for its furnishing not the country's *annals*, but the *perennials*, which are without date and hark back to the most primitive times (I, 230, 231).

Of "white man's poetry," that is, of literature as a conscious creation, Thoreau singles out some of the oldest as preferable to him — and
for the same reasons that he likes the vocabulary of Henry and the Indians. Homer is a favorite here, and Thoreau says he writes with
"naturalness" too: "it is as if nature spoke" (I, 94). Homer's descriptions, ever concrete, make Thoreau fancy, for example, that he hears
again the Minyas River discharging its waters into the ocean, hears
both the subdued murmur of the river and the hollow crash of the
ocean's waves. That Homer's subject is myth links his writing even
further to what is primitive. Thoreau describes myth as "unconscious
thoughts," something felt but not abstractly stated, and we already
noted in Chapter 3 that he equates such unconsciousness with that
supreme wildness, the consciousness of God. In sensuous terms, he
refers to myth as the "music" of thought, an approach to "universal
language" that contains only enduring truth (I, 58). It is a statement of
one's "oldest and finest memory" (I, 101), and he believes that no other
literature so adequately expresses a yearning for the wild (V, 232).

Of those poets writing in his own language, Thoreau calls Chaucer
the English Homer. His is the poetry of "life, rather than of thought,"
Thoreau says, reminding one of flowers blooming, birds singing, and
hearts beating (I, 393) — all things that appeal to the senses. Chaucer
also writes with "exceeding naturalness" (I, 398), preferring his homely, vigorous Saxon tongue to the more sophisticated language of the
court. With regard to vocabulary, Chaucer is like the seventeenth-
century religious writers, both in England and in America, whom
Thoreau admires as well. Thoreau's comments about them are in effect
a description of his own writing style. Francis Quarles, the Jacobean
emblematist in verse, uses, according to Thoreau, "able-bodied and
strong-backed words . . . which have a certain rustic fragrance and
force" (VII, 548). And John Bunyan's *Pilgrim's Progress*, 1678–84, with
its plain language and vivid images, is the best sermon ever preached
on the Bible, he claims.

Of New England's Puritan writers, Thoreau says that they use a
strong, homely speech "which brings you very near to the thing itself
described"; "they speak like men who have backs and stomachs and
bowels, with all the advantages that attach to them" (XIII, 109). In a
similar fashion he praises an early botanist, John Gerard, whose accounts

he prefers to those of many nineteenth-century naturalists. To Thoreau, Gerard seems really to have seen, tasted, and smelled his subject himself and then reported these sensations. In writing, as in economy, Thoreau sees that a division of labor would have ill effects: only those who pick their own huckleberries can really write about them. If one picks the berries, and another cooks them, while yet another writes about the experience, the account will be worthless, having no "spirit of the huckleberry in it" (XX, 295). Thoreau maintains as well that the labor involved in picking the berries tends to remove palaver from one's style.

It is often with the greatest economy of words that Thoreau himself can appeal strongly to our senses. Considering sundry examples from his own writing, we see that he relies upon various techniques to make us newly aware of some natural phenomenon. One is to relate that phenomenon to the human condition; for instance, the spring landscape is described as having a "green blush" (XIV, 243), and the evening red is seen as the color of the heel of departing day (VII, 152). A reason for nature's importance to him is in its reflection of man (XV, 121), and therefore it is normal for Thoreau to humanize the natural scene, particularly Walden Pond, whose depths he equates with his own soul (previously referred to in Chapter 2). The water is "earth's eye," in which the beholder can make soundings of his own nature (II, 206). Another pond, we are told, is nature's "blue navel" (XVIII, 378). If the entire landscape is seen as man, then other phenomena may be pictured as human artifacts: trees leafing out are summer "pitching its tent" (XI, 149); a snowbunting is a "winged snowball" (XII, 34); and, Thoreau puns, soaring hawks are "kites without strings" (X, 353).

Thoreau adopts additional techniques, in being economical with words, which allow his style to be termed sensuous. Because of his broad acquaintance with nature, he sometimes seems to assume that the same situation is true of his readers. What results are images that might be called over-concise. They achieve great impact—if they do not need to be explained first. "Finger-cold" (VII, 108), for example, is obvious enough. It describes finger-chilling weather. But *washing-day* (X, 131) is confusing, unless we know that he is referring to the clarity of the atmosphere. In other images over-conciseness speaks even more to the imagination, prompting a variety of suggestions and compelling the reader to partake in the creative process. Such is the case in Thoreau's description of autumn as "Indian warfare . . . waged through the forest" (V, 3). The image works because of the associations called up. "Indian warfare" suggests the redness of natives, of flaming arrows, and of bloodshed. At the same time there is a feeling of turmoil and riot, the sensation which he apparently believes occurs in one at the sight of autumn foliage.

Several of Thoreau's expressions are best described as showing a childlike perception. One such illustration is that of a bluebird carrying "the sky on his back" (IX, 386). He holds the romantic notion that the child possesses fresh insights into our world, and Thoreau retains some of this ingenuous wonder himself. Snow to him is the "sweeping of heaven's floor" (XIV, 89), and pines being bent over from the weight of snow are elbows stuck up under a sheet (XVII, 389).

Rural speech is often unsophisticated enough to have something of this same flavor, with perhaps greater homeliness and vigor. Thoreau realizes this fact, and compliments to the speech of New England countrymen are common in his writings. Scholars seldom write as well as a farmer talks, he says; or, sentences from rude hands have the quality of deer sinews and of pine roots; or, the surliness of a wood-chopper speaking of his own woods is better than the flowery utterances of a "nature lover." Since Thoreau prefers conversation with farmers Minott and Edmund Hosmer to that of refined society in town, many of his expressions are in their down-to-earth idiom. For example, a chub tastes like "boiled brown paper salted" (VIII, 16); chokeberries "fur the mouth" (XI, 387). In saying that wild apples have a "bow-arrow tang" (V, 310), an expression he learned from an old farmer, he jars us by substituting "tang" for the expected "twang," associated with bowstrings, and so conveys the shock of biting into a sour apple. "Arrow," meanwhile, is a fitting image to suggest the sharp taste.

When Thoreau finds existing speech inadequate, he coins new words. "What if there were a tariff on words, on language, for the encouragement of home manufacture?" he asks. "Have we not the genius to coin our own?" (XVIII, 390). He sees a need for distinctly American words to delineate American conditions: he would describe the course of his local river as *musketaquidding*, after its Indian name, rather than as *meandering*, after a classical river which also was serpentine. But he relies on any distinct words, whatever their place of origin, if they describe his environment in the way it speaks to his senses. He uses two rare coinages, for instance, which can characterize a rainy day. One in "mizzling" (XII, 159), formed from "drizzling" and "misty," which refers to a rain that is steady and prolonged. The other is "brattling" (X, 444), which apparently signifies to him the *rattling* sound made by frozen drizzle on trees when it is *breaking* up and falling off.

Thoreau's sensuousness is apparent too in his description of living things. When he discovers that certain defective trees in Maine are called *konchus*, and not knowing the derivation of the word, he likes to fancy it is derived from *conch* "that it might signify the dead sound which the trees yield when struck" (III, 120). Another coinage, "sky-scrapers," which originally applied to tall-masted sailing schooners, he uses in a new way with a sensuous reference to a high-flying hawk (IX, 143). He coins a name for a second bird, the parula warbler (known at that time as the blue yellow-backed warbler or parti-colored warbler). He calls it a "tweezer-bird" (XII, 369). This term is much more descriptive than the established names, which have little to do with what is distinctive about the bird. Most warblers are variously colored, and this one's so-called "yellow back" is in fact green. "Tweezer," on the other hand, suggests the bird's rasping call. The term speaks to our ear as well as to our intellect.

Often Thoreau appeals to several senses at the same time as if there were no real distinction between them: willow catkins have a "yellow smell" (IX, 432); the colors of flowers are "spices" to the eye (XI, 212); a bobolink's song "bespatter[s]" a meadow with melody (XV, 398); moss is a kind of "eye-brush" (XVII, 296); thunder is "round and plump" (III, 261). Here we have a few examples of his synesthesia, where the stimulation produced on one of the five senses is described in terms of another sense.

There is no real evidence that Thoreau involuntarily senses things in this manner, that is, that his is a clinical synesthesia, for then there need be no apt resemblance between the obvious sensation and what it is described as being. A willow catkin might well have a smell of any other color besides that which suggests the yellow pollen covering it. Furthermore, while the examples cited so far all are metaphors, where a sensation is directly stated to be something else or to possess qualities pertaining to one of the other senses, most examples from Thoreau seem to point to a sophisticated literary device used to delineate the better the full impact upon the relevant sense — with, perhaps, a general heightening of the other senses and of his entire being. The comparison is a conscious one. Thus, the crackling of hemlock boughs in a fire is *like* "mustard to the ears" (XII, 134); a sparrow's song is as distinct *as* "a spark of fire shot into the forest" (III, 214); a shrike's chinking note *suggests* "much ice in the stream" (XVIII, 20). Clearly, Thoreau is searching for the most suitable literary image.

A study of a writer's synesthetic transfers, the shift of words from the vocabulary of one sense to another, tells us something about how his imagination works. With Thoreau, in a sample of forty synesthetic images, the subject in about two-thirds of them has to do with sounds, and two-thirds of that number derive their vocabulary from the sense of sight. Most of the remaining subjects are concerned with sight, while the sense of touch, thermal and tactile, provides a vocabulary for about one-third of the total transfers. In any literary synesthesia it is usual for the majority of transfers between two senses to have the vocabulary taken from the higher level of the sensorium. Thoreau's many examples of visual audition are "conventional" in this regard, since sight is at a higher level than sound.

Not only is visual terminology richer than acoustic terminology, but sight is Thoreau's dominant sense and so can provide him with needed imagery elsewhere. For example, the songs of returning birds particularly affect him each spring, and his exhilaration requires some unusual (synesthetic) imagery to express it adequately. The bluebird's trill is one song he refers to year after year in such terms. Its notes are visualized as "curls" (XI, 23) of sound. In 1853 they remind him of "so many corkscrews assaulting and thawing the torpid mass of winter" (XI, 23), in 1857 he says the air is a "foundry full of molds for casting bluebirds' warbles" (XV, 270), and in 1859 he speaks of "this little rill of melody flow[ing] a short way down the concave of the sky" (XVIII, 5).

Concerning the other main source of vocabulary for acoustic images, that of touch, we find Thoreau describing a blue jay's scream as "frozen music" (XII, 118). This image is not original with him—it goes back to French and German writers, Madame De Staël and Goethe, who used it with regard to architecture. Unlike these writers, Thoreau uses it to suggest not just an arrested quality but presumably the startling abruptness with which the bird's strident call breaks upon the senses. What we find is especially typical of him, however, is to make this general image much more concrete—as he does in this example: a cricket's chirring in the cool of evening is the "*iced*-cream of song" (XII, 327).

Some of Thoreau's best short descriptions do not rely on some unusual image but rather on just the right word in its right place. Several references to birds provide characteristic illustrations. In referring to redpolls in these terms—"tropical colors, crimson breasts, on cold white snow!" (XIV, 42)—he is not only contrasting colors but also suggesting how incredible delicate birds with lively and social feeding habits seem against a background of winter's sterility. In similar fashion, but perhaps not as successful because his terminology is less concrete, he describes the pine grosbeak: "birds of paradise, dainty-footed, downy-clad, in the midst of a New England, a Canadian winter" (XIV, 43). Also noteworthy is this description of a purple finch: "many a serene evening lies snugly packed under its wing" (XII, 449). In these few words he implies that its plumage has taken on the crimson hues of a sunset and possibly that it takes satisfaction in flying at that time of day. Two further examples describe the sensation of flying in other ways. A bittern is pictured as "carr[ying] its precious legs away to deposit them in a place of safety" (I, 17). We can appreciate here something of the bird's labored flight, its long legs trailing conspicuously behind it. In another instance he makes us sense the majesty of a hawk's flight without actually describing that flight: "It . . . made all the earth lonely beneath it" (II, 349).

Thoreau always does praise a simple writing style because of the force and precision of plain statements. However, he finds that a simple style, even embodying his concise images, is not always rich enough for adequate expression: "Who will undertake to describe in words the difference in tint between two neighboring leaves on the same tree?" he asks (XVII, 255). Nature has a "luxurious and florid style" (VII, 271) of its own, and a similar one on his part seems called for. He needs to exaggerate, to write, as he says, *without* bounds, in order to give a true delineation.[5] If the "recognition by man of the least natural fact, and the allying his life to it," may be, as Thoreau claims, "*inex-pressibly beautiful*" (V, 20) [my italics], then the writer, by all means, needs to use whatever style is available to him in order to describe the effect best. He may need to "cut a broad swath" *and* "shave close" (II, 101), if necessary. We see in Thoreau's own writing style, then, the pro-fuse strain as well as the succinct phrase, and the distinctive flavor of his writing really results from both these features of style, complementing each other, working together to leave sensuous impressions.

In the following sentence from *The Maine Woods*, both sparseness and elaboration are evident: "The trees are a *standing* night, and every fir and spruce which you fell is a plume plucked from the night's raven-wing" (III, 303) [Thoreau's italics]. If the brief first clause seems to have a greater sensuous appeal than the longer succeeding clause because of the concise image of "*standing* night," the embellishments of the second clause help to clarify the meaning of the first and so give it impact. "*Standing* night" comes to suggest not only darkness but a lurking presence which surrounds and towers over one. Thoreau realizes that "standing" is a key word and rightly italicizes it, but it is the reference to "every" tree which increases our sense of this presence while the image of "raven" gives it its real, dark and ominous quality. An accumulation or an elaboration of precise images, a more extrav-agant style, conveys the meaning which some natural phenomenon has for him.

Much of what Thoreau writes deals with his own walks and excur-sions so that it already has a kind of discursiveness appropriate to his rambles. He makes copious notes outdoors—for example, on a rail fence during a moonlit night—and captures the immediacy of the scene in sensuous terms. In this instance the moonlight shines on his paper, and his pencil, he says, seems to move through a mystic me-dium, greatly different from that found indoors by a sunlit table: the moonlight is "rich and opaque, like cream" (while daylight is "thin and blue, like skimmed milk") (XI, 278). What he usually does, however, in trying to treat an event fully, is to allow some lapse in time before describing it—while he advocates writing when the "heat" is in one (IX, 293), such time, we find, need not be the moment of original perception when the heat is greatest. His art is nature passed through the alembic of man: he "taste[s] the world and digest[s] it" (IX, 85), makes it a part of him, in order to say something adequately. As in the British Romantic poets, spontaneity is really characteristic of the *origin* of a work for him.

A second procedure which Thoreau adopts, related to the first, is to make two or more reports in his *Journal*. Doing so gains for him an additional perspective, as if he were seeing a landscape once more with his head inverted. Each revision or new report becomes an expanded sensation, leading to new insights. In one such instance the color of a patch of dwarf andromeda excites him, and his repeated descriptions of it extend over several days. He first calls the color a "grayish-brown hue tinged with red"; then he sees it as a "charming warm, what I call *Indian*, red color, the mellowest, the ripest, red imbrowned color"; finally he calls it a "warm, rich red tinge, surpassing cathedral windows" (IX, 430). A few days later he recalls the andromeda, and feeling that his former descriptions are incomplete, he adds still more to them: "These little leaves are . . . stained windows . . . . At sight of any redness I am excited like a cow" (IX, 442).

What we find emerging in Thoreau's finished essays, which after all grow out of his journal entries, are descriptions which capture the essentialness of the experience, ones which in their flow of words keep a kind of balance between excess and order. He numbers all the streaks of the tulip[6] because, having done so, he is the better able to select those which are its distinguishing features, those which will convey the desired impression to the reader. For example, in "A Winter Walk," he wishes to impress upon the reader that the air is cold. He does so not by merely repeating this fact among other descriptive material but by using a more complex kind of repetition. He pictures the air again and again as a purified and as a near solid substance. Both characteristics, apparently, are supposed to suggest the low temperatures. Thus he speaks of "the stiffened air exploring the dawn," and in the next paragraph he continues as follows: "The withdrawn and tense sky seems groined like the aisles of a cathedral, and the polished air sparkles." Only a solid object, we note, can be "polished." The paragraph concludes with a reference to "this pure stinging cold" as a "crystalized midsummer haze." But the redescribing has not ended. Two paragraphs later he talks of the "cleansed air" being "visible to the eye" and, four paragraphs later still, of the air being "refined and shrunk by the chaste winter's cold" (V, 165–169). By this time the reader is beginning to feel chilled to his very marrow.

It is the accumulative effect of sensuous terms in "Wild Apples," carefully chosen once more but this time incorporated into a single paragraph, which makes Thoreau's description of the fruit "delicious" (Thoreau would approve the use of this last term):

> Painted by the frost, some a uniform clear bright yellow, or red, or crimson, as if their spheres had regularly revolved, and enjoyed the influence of the sun on all sides alike, — some with the faintest pink blush imaginable, — some brindled with deep red streaks, like a cow, or with hundreds of fine blood-red rays running regularly from the stem-dimple to the blossom end, like meridional lines, on a straw-colored ground, — some touched with a greenish rust, like a fine lichen, here and there, with crimson blotches or eyes more or less confluent and fiery when wet, — and others gnarly, and freckled or peppered all over on the stem side with fine crimson spots on a white ground, as if accidentally sprinkled from the brush of Him who paints the autumn leaves. Others, again, are sometimes red inside, perfused with a beautiful blush, fairy food, too beautiful to eat, — apple of the Hesperides, apple of the evening sky! (V, 314–315)

Here, there is a feeling of abundance, not only of apples but of their various colors. The repetition of "some" (four times) and of "others" (twice) creates a kind of balance as the ordered account unfolds and at the same time gives the illusion of great variety. However, it is the disposition of the colors on each apple which has more sensuous appeal than the colors themselves. The apples are bright or pale, brindled or rayed or freckled. If they are blotched, the blotches may be scattered or confluent. In some the color extends within — is "perfused" throughout the apple. Always Thoreau is looking for comparisons, repeating "like . . ." and "as if . . . ," in order to describe the effect. He seems overwhelmed and must end the paragraph with three appositives, reaching into the mystery and antiquity of Greek myth.

Elsewhere Thoreau uses the technique of elaboration for creating specific contrasts and also for providing a kind of parallelism. In one instance he seems deliberately to overwhelm us with warm colors in a description of a sunset so that the ensuing cool blue of the changing sky will be as refreshing to us as it is to him: "There was a warm sunset over the wooded valleys, a yellowish tinge on the pines. Reddish dun-colored clouds like dusky flames stood over it. And then streaks of blue sky were seen here and there. The life, the joy, that is in blue sky . . ." (VIII, 138). In another instance he attempts to describe the liquid song of a red-winged blackbird by referring to melodic things of a kindred nature—a "musical water-pipe," a "liquid bagpipe or clarionet," and a "hurried, gurgling fugue" (XI, 91). In a separate journal entry, his search for verbs to delineate the progress of this song has itself something in it of the liquid quality of the strain: "It oozes, trickles, bubbles from his throat" (IX, 457).

Thoreau has an ear for the music of nature. If he wants to march according to the grand rhythm of the universe, his prose keeps time to its lesser periods. His account of the squirrels in *Walden*, with all its parenthetical phrases and clauses, goes by fits and starts to parallel the movements of the squirrels. In evoking these complex sensations of the animal movement, he engages our sensuous empathy with an appeal to our kinesthetic sense. Our muscles seem to tense in imitation of the "dance" of one of the squirrels, as much as though we were listening to actual music. That he is deliberately manipulating rhythms and images to cause this effect is made obvious by his comparison of the squirrel to a dancing girl:

One would approach at first warily through the shrub oaks, running over the snow-crust by fits and starts like a leaf blown by the wind, now a few paces this way, with a wonderful speed and waste of energy, making inconceivable haste with his "trotters," as if it were for a wager, and now as many paces that way, but never getting on more than half a rod at a time; and then suddenly pausing with a ludicrous expression and a gratuitous somerset as if all the eyes in the universe were fixed on him, —for all the motions of a squirrel, even in the most solitary recesses of the forest, imply spectators as much as those of a dancing girl, — wasting more time in delay and circumspection than would have sufficed to walk the whole distance, — I never saw one walk, — and then suddenly, before you could say Jack Robinson, he would be in the top of a young pitch pine, winding up his clock and chiding all imaginary spectators, soliloquizing and talking to all the universe at the same time, — for no reason that I could ever detect, or he himself was aware of, I suspect. (II, 302)

The asides to the reader, which interrupt this sentence of some 200 words, seem to prolong the fidgety activity of the squirrel. The elaboration, we should note, also extends outside the sentence, for two similar lengthy ones follow it in *Walden*.

Later in the book when Thoreau writes of the flowing sand and clay of a thawing cutbank, his description rhythmically imitates what is happening. He fills the passage with words ending in *ing* since their very sound suggests flowing — while the sound of such phrases as "laciniated, lobed, and imbricated thalluses" (II, 336) might suggest the interlacing of the streams. He says elsewhere that sentences should palpitate, should have blood under their rinds which gives them life. His sentences describing the flowing sand have this quality. But then he also traces the progress of the streams to their becoming flatter strands, flat sandy reaches, and finally newly formed banks. In so doing, he slows down the pace of his prose by interjecting such words as "gradually" and "almost" and also the curt-sounding "flat" and "broad" (II, 337).

As well as hearing the "meaning" of words with his ear, Thoreau seems even to feel the "meaning" with his lips as he writes them down. By taking them on his lips, he says in the *Journal*, the words become a product of the lips. The words "edacious" and "voracious," for example, refer to "not nibbling and swallowing merely, but eating and swallowing while the lips are greedily collecting more food," since the lips must be protruded in pronouncing the Latin termination *cious* (VIII, 443). In *Walden* (II, 337–340), he investigates this overall notion further. He is using two main images in describing the flowing sandbank, that of foliage and that of vitals, and suggesting the movement

elaborations seem to represent the succeeding moments of his sensed experience so that the movement of the writing simulates his ongoing response. We, the readers, are made to sense his full awareness of the world immediately around him. It is this closeness to the natural world, this lack of objectivity, however, which becomes a hindrance to his following any scientific bent.

6 An Appointment with a Beech Tree

Thoreau's encounter with a woodchuck, described in the *Journal* for April 16, 1852 (IX, 420–423), shows his strengths and limitations as a naturalist. One strength is his contact with the *living* world of nature rather than with dead specimens, for he spends much time outdoors. In this instance he spies the first woodchuck of the season and runs along a fence to head it off and then overtakes it, the animal stopping and facing its pursuer. He now proceeds to describe the woodchuck in a detailed manner, having ample time, he tells us, to make observations. The fence, we note, is literally and symbolically between them, and Thoreau gives us an objective account. We learn even the color and length of the animal's whiskers. He also includes a few question marks after some observations in his wish to be scrupulously accurate. Giving this kind of full and precise record is a mark of a good naturalist.

After a half page of such description, however, Thoreau's objectivity falls away; he reaches through the fence with a twig, using it to play "tenderly" with the woodchuck. Such involvement could be a strength if it would lead to a recording of more worthwhile scientific facts. But with him the exercise takes on value chiefly for its own sake. His approach as a naturalist is limited because his personal response rather than the subject under study becomes of prime importance. He writes: "We sat looking at one another about half an hour, till we began to feel mesmeric influences." Although he will yet make a few objective statements—for example, about the woodchuck's paws—his examination is carried out "at pleasure."

Thoreau ends the encounter by patting the animal and comes away not so much with some new scientific knowledge but with a feeling that he might learn some wisdom from the woodchuck by means of an empathic insight into its life. The animal with its "terrestrial color," he feels, is "naturalized" amid the withered grass and bushes, more thoroughly so than he is. Its species had to be conversant with things, to be sensible of them, over a long period of time in order to acquire through adaptation the color of the place. Thoreau then observes else-where — with some profundity — that an animal's protective coloration shows the creature's unity with the earth. However, he has no ac-cumulated evidence, as in a scientific investigation, to support his con-clusion. And we find that an empathic attempt to be sensible of the world, as individual constituents of nature are, may also cause misconceptions. In another instance it prompts him to observe — we think not so profoundly this time — that a decayed leaf which reveals its network of veins might be a repulsive skeleton to its fellow members of the vegetable kingdom.[1]

Thoreau's work as a naturalist, with its limitations or strengths, is always closely related to his sensuousness. His sensuous concern can be a spur to his study of nature, but this same concern gives him a casual attitude towards measurement and a distrust of scientific instruments which supposedly abet the senses. Also, sensuousness affects his success as an ornithologist and a botanist; yet since it makes him delight in nature's survival of the fittest, he is ahead of his time in his interest in interrelationships in nature. Finally, his several arguments with con-temporary science have a sensuous basis as he gives emphasis to his own subjective response to natural phenomena.

Thoreau's sensuous involvement with nature often gives rise to a scientific investigation. If he can dip his hand into a lake to lift out breams for observation, it is because he has allowed them to nibble his fingers. In another instance, his sensuous delight in nature prompts him to examine myriads of air bubbles in the ice at Walden Pond. He marvels at their varied shapes and describes them as "very clear and beautiful." However, having examined so many of them, he can "infer," in the true scientific fashion of induction, that they operate as burning glasses to melt the ice and make it crack and whoop (II, 273–274).

Sometimes he *combines* a sensuous description with one that is also scientifically informative, such as his comment on the geological maturing of rivers: "in the course of ages the rivers wriggle in their beds, till [each bed] feels comfortable under them" (XIII, 268). His sensuous concern, we find, may not only initiate a scientific study but prolong it as well. It is the bruising of his hand on a rock that starts his investigation of lichens on it, and he spends an entire rainy afternoon closely scrutinizing them. This study, as he describes it in the *Journal*, continues also to be a sensuous activity, however: "To study lichens is to get a taste of earth. . . . The lichenist loves the tripe of the rock, — that which eats and digests the rocks. He eats the eater. . . . There is no . . . salve for sore eyes as these brightening lichens on a moist day" (XVII, 440).

There are, of course, accounts by Thoreau which seem solely devoted to science. The best known of these is his "Succession of Forest Trees," in which he calls himself a "naturalist" and says that the essay is on a "purely scientific subject" (V, 185). Its technical value is evidenced by its being listed later in E. N. Munns's *Selected Bibliography of North American Forestry*, 1940; yet Thoreau's interest in the topic, we shall see, seems to be again a part of his sensuous concern. The essay explains why pines spring up when an oak wood is cut down and why the process is reversed should a stand of pines be chopped away, provided that both trees are common to the area. He finds that the seeds of both trees are planted annually, that pine seedlings are more abundant and therefore hold a natural advantage over the oak seedlings, but that the latter are nurtured in the shelter and shade of a pine woods better than the little pines themselves, thus gaining a headstart there on their rivals. He is scientific in testing his theory in case after case before he makes his findings public. Still, such testing is allied with his interest in the management of woodlots which, paradoxically, he is sometimes asked to survey so that the owner might cut them down. Thoreau writes: "I despair of my trees, — I say mine, for the farmer evidently does not mean that they shall be his" (XX, 145). This interest of his in turn grows out of his love of wilderness areas; every town, he maintains, should have a park, or better yet, a primitive forest where one can enjoy nature.

Thoreau's real interest in oak seedlings seems apparent from his passionate, although not humorless, description of a shrub oak (XV, 145–148). The "dear wholesome color" of its leaves, which "rustl[e] like leather shields," are fair to the eye, smooth to the touch. Because of the "positive yearning" he harbors toward the oak, he loves to walk straight through a stand of these trees, feeling the branches tear at his clothes and scratch his face. An oak is for him something to embrace, to fall in love with. As for his interest in the conservation of the birds which inhabit the woodlots, that too has its sensuous basis. In enunciating a plea that natural beauty, being really a public heritage, should be preserved for its own sake, he maintains that legislatures need to regard not only the "low use" of birds—the contents of their crops, but the "high use"—the "beauty of their plumage" and the "sweetness of their song" (XVIII, 124).

Indeed, each of Thoreau's scientific reports is seen to be complemented by some sensuous account of the same subject, showing the overriding nature of sensuousness in his habitual thought even with regard to those subjects which lend themselves particularly to scientific disquisition. His detailed description of the mechanics of a toad's croaking in the *Journal* has its counterpart in the well-known passage from *Walden* where frogs are treated as unrepentant wassailers. Whereas the toad "gulp[s]" wind into its belly in order to swell out its throat-soundbox (X, 25), the frogs "gulp" not air but liquor into distended paunches as the flowing bowl is passed along with a *"tr-r-r-oonk"* (II, 140).

Again, when Thoreau finds a wounded sucker, he takes it home, weighs and measures it, gives a precise account of its coloring, describes the nostrils in its "gibbous" head, tells how far apart the eyes are, counts the number of scales along the lateral line, and then counts the rays in each fin (XII, 460). He implies elsewhere that it is his love of fishes that makes him wish to know every detail about them. Facts are only a frame to his picture of nature, although, since they speak of nature, they are also of importance in themselves. But when he discovers a new species of fish in Walden Pond, he treats the discovery in an entirely unscientific manner. He says he cannot go beyond exulting in the miracle of the fish's existence—and does only that for three pages of the *Journal* in the following fashion: "I cannot but see still in my mind's eye those little striped breams poised in Walden's glaucous water. . . . I can only think of precious jewels, of music, poetry, beauty, and the mystery of life . . ." (XVII, 358–360). Thoreau does not care to measure the fish's length or weight, only its beauty.

Although Thoreau's later journals show more and more reports based on measurement, his attitude toward measurement remains somewhat nonchalant. In spite of its being a principal feature of the scientific method, its use by him is more or less an aside to his sensuous response to nature. Thus, it is his walking stick on which he rules out twenty-four inches to measure some phenomenon of nature when he saunters out each day. In 1853 when he makes his second excursion to the Maine woods, he neglects to take any measuring instrument with him at all. He must use a canoe's painter to take measurements of a moose that has been killed, making a knot in the cord for each measurement. So that the cord may again be used for what it was intended, he changes these measurements to lengths and fractions of his umbrella, untying the knots as he proceeds. He takes all these pains, he tells us, "because I did not wish to be obliged to say merely that the moose was very large" (III, 126). To Thoreau, we noted in Chapter 3, the moose epitomizes wildness, and he wishes to be able to catch something of this quality in specific terms with regard to the animal's huge size. On a following day, he finally obtains a ruler and converts the "umbrella" measurements to feet and inches. He also makes a two-foot ruler of his own, making it from a native black ash, and for this he does find "constant use" (III, 141) as the wilderness excursion proceeds.

Thoreau tends to favor a measuring instrument that seems the least artificial, one that is made from material which is somehow related to what the instrument will measure. Such an instrument is a connecting link to nature, not a mere tool. To measure a river's depth, he notes in 1859, a heron's leg is the most fitting instrument; the heron has already used it to sound the water on every bar along the shore. It has served the bird's sense of touch, and Thoreau, we are led to believe, would like to think it may serve as an extension of this same sense in man.

Like the heron, Thoreau shares an interest in water conditions, in Thoreau's case those of Concord River, of local springs, and of Walden Pond, and he measures them assiduously. His approach is largely scientific here, but sensuous considerations tend to creep into his investigations even though he expresses his interest in a scientist's phraseology, in feet and inches rather than in heron's tibiae. It is he who suggests that the town erect a stone marker in the river, graduated in inches, and have someone record each high or low water level. In 1859 he, at the town's request, spends more than a month studying the physiography of the river, compiling detailed tables of statistics on its fluctuating depths, its current speed, and the like. From his observations he comes to conclusions such as the following—"the presence or absence of weeds at a given shallowness is a good gauge of the rapidity of the current" (XVIII, 255)—and provides specific illustrations. At the same time he finds it a unique experience to recline on those weeds which form a dense mat on a muddy pool once the water level goes down, calling them "quite agreeable to rest on and a rather novel sight" (XVIII, 278).

In the following year Thoreau carries a thermometer about with him each afternoon for an entire week in order to ascertain the temperature of springs in his area. This activity leads him to speculate why most of them are located at the base of a bank or hill on the edge of river or meadow: "apparently the water which percolates through the hill or upland, having reached a stratum saturated with water and impervious to it, bursts out in a spring" (XIX, 389). This inference has a practical application in locating a water supply, for he adds, "An indefinite number of such springs may be found and cleared out" (XIX, 389–390). Some of those which he examined are known to him alone, and he clears them out annually, as part of his faithful (and unpaid) employment as "overseer" of Concord township. Such occupation, referred to in *Walden*, appeals to his sensuous nature. His further measurement of temperatures—at various depths of Walden Pond— has been described as an "original and genuine" contribution to science and earn for him the title of "first American limnologist."[2] He measures the temperature at the warm surface and at the hundred-foot level and finds that the lower depth gives the same reading as does a cold spring. The temperature differences between levels, he concludes, will affect fish distribution.

Still, Thoreau can be considered a scientist only at intervals. His measurements do not always point to a conclusion, do not always have any real scientific value. When he measures a white oak blown down by the wind, his measurements are casually descriptive—the length of the tree, its breadth, the diameter of the roots, the circumference at the five-foot mark. On the other hand, when he counts the number of tree rings in each inch of radius of several pitch pines, he concludes at what age these trees reach their peak in rate of growth. Such information has ramifications for the forest industry. Futhermore, with his study he anticipates what scientists will later do in using growth patterns for dating ancient sites, for he writes: "I can not only detect the order of events but the time during which they elapsed, by counting the rings of the stumps. Thus you unroll the rotten papyrus on which the history of the Concord forest is written" (XX, 152). He pursues his study with such vigor, even on the bitterest of winter days, that he contracts the cold which marks the onset of his final illness. His measurements, then, may or may not be scientifically significant. What is common to them is their being a means of giving concreteness to his sensuous appreciation of what is being measured, as shown in the following incident. When an old Concord elm is felled, his praise of the venerable giant is in the measuring of it: "I have taken the measure of his grandeur" (XIV, 130), he says. The action itself is a kind of affectionate touch.

Thoreau has little use for scientific instruments which tend to separate him physically from the subject studied. It is a sparrow within reach on his shoulder which distinguishes him and which makes him feel distinguished (II, 304). He wants to use his sense of touch in conjunction with his other senses. For this reason, an instrument he does rely upon frequently throughout his adult life is a magnifying glass or "microscope." Ordinarily he is already looking with "microscopic eye" into some phenomena of nature, such as the furrowed bark of a tree (I, 319). Magnifying things at hand does not remove him from them, does not cause him to lose a sensuous contact. Thus in order to examine with his microscope three of the combatants of the battle of the ants, described in *Walden*, he must actually bring them physically closer by lifting them onto his window sill.

But Thoreau finds he can look *too* close when, one winter, he discovers a patch of rose-colored ice. He immediately speculates what could have been the cause—muskrat blood? vegetable pigment? When he cannot be sure, he gives way to a sensuous exclamation: "This beautiful blushing ice!" Still, he goes out the next day with basket and hatchet and secures a "specimen" of it, which he examines with his magnifying glass. He discovers in the ice minute air bubbles coated with red dust and is somewhat wiser scientifically but concludes: "It has not beauty nor brightness thus seen" (XIII, 139, 142).

Thoreau's qualms about the use of a telescope, which makes *faraway* phenomena appear close, are much more pronounced than those about using the magnifying glass. He first considers buying one, according to the *Journal*, in March, 1853, thinking it the best means of studying shy birds such as hawks. Better to bring them nearer alive than nearer dead as a gun would do, he feels. That summer he borrows a spyglass and observes a distant hawk for all of an hour, exulting that he can now observe "how its eye and whole head express anger!" (XI, 235). The next spring he buys a telescope for himself. This purchase comes relatively late in his life, and he believes that by this time he will be prepared to make a perfect use of it. It is not long, however, before he objects to it. True, the glass would be considered of little value by to-day's bird watchers because of the difficulty in focusing, the poor illumination, and the narrow field of view. But Thoreau's objection is more fundamental: the spyglass brings only the eye close to the subject. Relying on this crutch, one may soon be farther from the subject than before. Also, the magnification makes the subject monstrous, unreal: "With our prying instruments we disturb the balance and harmony of nature" (XVIII, 171). That is why he seems to imply that the true man of science need rely on no other assistance but that provided by his own senses. The scientist "should be the healthiest man" (*LJ*, 171); "he will smell, taste, see, hear, feel, better than other men. . . . We do not learn by inference and deduction and the application of mathematics to philosophy but by direct intercourse and sympathy" (V, 131).

Thoreau's wish to rely on his senses alone may account for the several errors that he makes in his descriptions. Had he a telescope in 1853, he might not have thought that a ruffed grouse makes its drumming noise by beating its wings on a log (XI, 144–145). He here is more concerned with his own response to the sound than its origin, describing the beat as "veritable little drumsticks on our tympanum, as if it were a throbbing or fluttering in our veins or brows or the chambers of the ear, and belonging to ourselves." He also often confuses songs of two or more birds, it being likely that the bird he hears is not the bird he actually is seeing. Again, a telescope would have remedied the error. Thus in his *Journal* for May 4, 1853, he writes "chickadee," with reference to a song he has heard, crosses it out and substitutes "myrtle-bird," then makes a final correction to "white-throat sparrow." Neither does he distinguish clearly between the songs of the wood thrush and hermit thrush, although he rhapsodizes about them many times.

A further confusion applies to Thoreau's three mystery birds. His "seringo-bird" is usually the savannah sparrow, but with the aid of a telescope he would not have described it, for instance, as having both reddish-brown markings (as a fox sparrow has) and white in its tail (as a vesper sparrow has). His "evergreen-forest bird" on one occasion is the black-throated green warbler but generally the name is used with regard to any unknown bird song heard in the woods. His "night-warbler" crops up repeatedly in the *Journal*. After he buys his spyglass, he does once claim it to be a yellowthroat, but most often his descriptions of its song pertain to the ovenbird. He never does identify the bird positively, and Emerson advises him not to try, for then nature would hold less mystery for him. The "night warbler" remains for Thoreau a bird he would rather hold in his affections than in his hand. Its song ever gives wings to his imagination and heightens all his senses.

Thoreau's confusions about certain bird songs do not mean he is a casual listener or necessarily has a poor ear. Such conclusions would belie his sensuous nature. What we find instead is that his writings are filled with attempts to delineate the melody and rhythm of song after song — both by using actual words or by using imitative syllables. In *The Maine Woods*, syllables record the song of a white-throated sparrow in at least four different ways as though Thoreau were listening with fresh ears each time. It is the song which is important to him, more so than the positive identification of the bird. He might well have paraphrased Shakespeare: the song by any other bird would sound as sweet.

Most of the early criticism directed by naturalists at Thoreau was aimed specifically at his errors in bird study. Bradford Torrey, in his "Introduction" to the *Journal* (1906), belittles Thoreau's scientific achievement by pointing out that Thoreau did not know that the downy woodpecker was a winter bird nor did he observe the conspicuous rose-breasted grosbeak until 1853. John Burroughs, in "A Critical Glance into Thoreau" (1919), takes pains to point out the offences committed by Thoreau in ornithology, as well as in other branches of natural history. Unfortunately, literary critics have chosen to carry on this disparagement of Thoreau's science — from Norman Foerster's saying (1923) that any schoolboy in five short years could excel Thoreau in all he knew about birds, to Charles Anderson's claim (1971) that Thoreau's scientific studies are not of "much interest to the biologist today."[3]

But present-day scientists have changed their estimate of Thoreau's scientific investigations, so that now it is chiefly the literary critics who, strangely enough, really attempt to discredit his reputation in this field. Scientists today have a much broader perspective than they did in the nineteenth century, when many were engaged in the narrow task of classifying and naming the flora and fauna of the largely unexplored North American continent. Witness the fictional Dr. Obed Bat in James Fenimore Cooper's *The Prairie*, 1827. Scientists then jealously guarded their professional ranks from intrusion by nature lovers and sensuous Thoreauvians who were not as rigid and systematic as they were. Now with the increasing prestige of science of our own century, scientists feel no qualms about securing information from any source available, including Thoreau and his *Journal*, and ignore attempts by the literati to retain him exclusively for themselves. The *Journal* has become a valuable mine of scientific data: meteorologists delve into it for past weather patterns; ornithologists study it to analyze changing bird populations.[4]

Today's scientists now tend to minimize the errors in Thoreau's observations, errors which we have seen stem at least in part from his sensuousness. Helen Cruickshank, for example, who has edited a book of his bird observations,[5] is surprised that he identifies as many birds as he does, considering the reference books available to him, the chief being by John James Audubon and Alexander Wilson. Audubon in one instance lists a species of warbler under three separate names while both men state that the hermit thrush has no real song. It is for good reason then that Thoreau hears mystery warblers and usually calls all singing thrushes "wood" thrushes. As for the cause of the sound of a ruffed grouse's drumming, Cruickshank says that this was not definitely ascertained until revealed by slow-motion moving pictures. She feels that Thoreau is in advance of his time with some of his ideas — such as his tenable suggestion that birds may navigate by the stars during migration.

Of course some of Thoreau's notions, we find, which might have been unique in the mid-nineteenth century, when he wrote them down, were no longer so in 1906 when the complete *Journal* was finally published. A prime example relates to the system of a bird identification made internationally famous by the field guides of Roger Tory Peterson. They focus attention on how one bird species may be distinguished from another at a distance by its color pattern and outline. Peterson at first attributes the idea to Ernest Thompson Seton's book, *Two Little Savages*, which appeared in 1903. (Seton had originally broached the notion in an article in *The Auk* in 1897.) Yet credit is now given to Thoreau, who with his characteristic visual acuity discusses the same idea in his *Journal* in 1853 (XI, 188–189) and again in 1860 (XIX, 194). Thoreau's further observations have been acclaimed in areas other than ornithology — and limnology, which was referred to previously. Virginia Eifert — in *Tall Trees and Far Horizons*, 1965, a book detailing the work of such plant experts as Linnaeus, Andre Michaux, and Thomas Nuttall — has one chapter which she entitles simply, "The Botanist, Thoreau."

It is true that Thoreau makes a better botanist than an ornithologist. Usually, he can make direct contact with birds only when they are dead, and he does not like to take warm-blooded life. In this latter regard he is akin to many present-day naturalists, who prefer finding birds already dead to using their collectors' permits. He does once purposely shoot a junco to study it, but he sells his gun before moving to Walden Pond and thereafter chooses to study either living birds or, when he can find them, dead birds as well. Thus one bitterly cold day finds him crawling on his stomach over the frozen ground to get a close view of ducks on some water. Or another day finds him wishing that he could come upon a dead duck floating on the water so that he might examine it — and the next day, he is "delighted" to find a "perfectly fresh and very beautiful" merganser. He writes a four-page detailed and glowing description of it in his *Journal*, studded with technical terms and having references to Nuttall and Wilson (XIII, 287–291).

With a living bird in hand, however, Thoreau's prime concern is with the "aliveness" of the bird, and his response, ever sensuous, tends to be defined by this single quality. His examination, we see, may then be limited or even postponed indefinitely. Thus, when he captures a screech owl and takes it home for a night the better to observe it, his description, also four pages in length, is not so comprehensive but instead focuses upon what he feels is the essence of this living creature — its "great solemn eyes" (XIII, 522–525). On a different occasion when he finds another screech owl, in a hole in a tree, he cuts short his investigation altogether: "After a little while I put in one hand and stroked it repeatedly whereupon it reclined its head a little lower and closed its eye entirely. Though curious to know what was under it, I disturbed it no farther at that time" (XIII, 365).

With plants, Thoreau does not feel so much the intruder. Botanizing, he can use all his senses — seeing, smelling, touching, and tasting the plants in the field as well as hearing the wind rustle through them. Although he says at one point that he prefers not to pick flowers, liking them best outdoors, he does in fact show little compunction about plucking them, and his third trip to the Maine woods is to a large part a botanizing expedition. His usual method of collecting plants is to stuff them under his hat for carrying home. By pulling the lining partly down to form a shelf, he has a "botany-box" (X, 133), the success of which depends upon his own physical presence, for he feels that the warmth and dampness there, generated by walking, preserve the flowers.

At home Thoreau can examine the plants further and delight in his collection. One of his favorites is the water lily, with which he amuses himself by blowing through the pores of its stem in order to observe its yellow stamens fluttering. He also floats one in a pan of water and watches its pure white petals spring open at his touch. The breath of his admiration, he says, makes it sail across the dish. On one of his field trips, he finds a toadstool as big as his hat, but the plant is so delicate that he must hold it upright to bring home, paddling his boat with one hand while he does so. He gives the plant his usual sensuous inspection, noting that as he looks up within it, the light is transmitted between its trembling gills. Early the next morning (7:30 a.m.) he is showing off his prize on the streets of Concord.

Thoreau's wish is, as he says, to get nearer the plants, to know them as neighbors (XV, 157). He often visits plants half a dozen times in a space of two weeks, walking four or five miles on each occasion in order to catch them at the height of bloom and so gratify his sense of sight. At the same time he expects to see plants very foreign to the locality and finds at length that he surely does see them, thus adding a score or more of rare plants as new "neighbors." So proficient is he in his activities here that he says if he woke up from a trance in a nearby swamp, he could tell the date within two days simply by noting what plants were blooming. In one instance a fellow townsman discovers the whereabouts of a plant, the pink azalea, before he does. When the man proves reluctant to give its location, Thoreau terms himself a botanist and therefore insists that he be told. If he is not, he will, he says, search the district and find it himself, for he can "smell" it from a considerable distance (XI, 206). When he is shown the plant, he speaks of its color and fragrance, as we would expect, and also of its *clamminess*! He is indeed a sensuous botanist.

Thoreau continues his visits to plants throughout the year, not only when they are blossoming. He walks some ten miles through deep snow to keep an appointment with a beech tree. He describes studying hoarfrost on plants as a kind of winter "botany" which he enjoys. By saying that the grasses in this season seem "hung with innumerable jewels, which jingle merrily as they [are] brushed by the foot" (V, 126, 127), he suggests that the sensuous appeal of the activity — of any botanizing, for that matter — has always been a prime attraction to him.

A strict adherence to the rigid systematizing practiced by contemporary botanists, on the other hand, Thoreau finds somewhat artificial and confining. But greater attention to this practice might have eliminated the few confusions that appear in his own accounts, such as his early uncertainty in distinguishing white spruce from black. It is a demonstration linked to sensuousness which finally brings home the difference to him: in 1857 his Indian guide in the Maine woods strokes a twig of each tree and points out that the needles of one do not stand at the same angle as those on the other. Thoreau likes this explanation, it relating "both to sight and touch" (II, 225). If we find Thoreau's method of dealing with plants here, and elsewhere, to be rather personal, his botanical study, scientific and/or sensuous in approach, is a concrete achievement: at his death he leaves more than a thousand specimens of pressed plants to the Boston Society of Natural History.

Thoreau's listing of plants in habitat groups, as in the appendix to *The Maine Woods*, shows that he is interested in the relationship among various phenomena of nature — among plants and animals and the earth and climate in which they live. Just as he wishes to use all his senses, so he wishes to apply them to all nature. He cannot narrow to one discipline his approach to nature. Instead he tends to become infatuated by one natural phenomenon for a certain time and temporarily gives himself over to its study, feeding his senses on it, becoming acquainted with it in all its aspects. For example, 1853 is a year in which he concentrates on studying birds' nests, while the winter of 1855–56 marks his interest in the phenomenon of snow — its depths, its drifts, its colors, as well as the animal tracks it reveals.

Thoreau's chief interest for a single month, that of April, 1858, makes that interval aptly termed his frog month. He is out every day observing these creatures by wading in the watery meadows and rivers, in the spring pools and ditches. There is one report of his standing stock-still in the water for several hours studying a bullfrog. Sometimes he sits down at the brink of a pond and waits till the frog becomes curious about *him*, so curious that it hops in his direction. "Perchance you may now scratch its nose with your finger and examine it to your heart's content" (XVI, 375), he says. In this month of April, he writes many accounts of the appearance of frogs and of their croaking, mating, and laying of spawn. He notes how they choose, "not accidentally" (XVI, 375), the habitat where they deposit the spawn and notes also how they respond to temperatures.

Because of this kind of many-faceted approach by Thoreau, his findings perhaps have more value to ecology than to any other branch of science. The word is not coined till after his death, so that his broad approach, shaped by his sensuousness, is not really appreciated by scientists until well on into our own century. Edward S. Deevey, Jr., may have been the first (1942) to call him an ecologist, but others have taken up this notion, Philip and Kathryn Whitford calling him a "pioneer" in the field.[6] Even Thoreau's statement in *Walden* about a mouse completely gnawing around a pitch pine at his hut and so killing it has its ecological basis. He reflects that the occurrence of the little animal thus being allowed to have a whole pine tree for its meal may be necessary "in order to thin these trees, which are wont to grow up

densely" (II, 309). Also concerned with interrelationships is the journal passage which points out that a half-open pasture in the woods is
abandoned to one species of bird alone, the field sparrow. Thoreau
speaks of a "beautiful law of distribution" which makes this fact possible and adds that as the pines increase the thrushes will take its place.
Typically, this reflection is prompted by an appeal to his senses, his
hearing the "jingle" of these sparrows in the pasture (XVIII, 154–155).

Thoreau's wish to make an atlas or calendar of nature's total economy
at Concord—embracing geography, climate, plant and animal life—
also relates to ecology—and to his sensuous response to the cycle of
seasonal change. He writes: "Why should I hear the chattering of
blackbirds, why smell the skunk each year? . . . I would at least
know what these things unavoidably are, make a chart of our life,
know how its shores trend, that butterflies reappear and when, know
just why this circle of creatures completes the world" (IX, 438). The
data dealing with climatic influences on such annual phenomena as
bird migrations and budding, all of which he collects in his *Journal* for
this proposed calendar, shows his kinship with Gilbert White of Britain
and earns for him yet another citation from a scientist of our century.
Aldo Leopold calls him the "father of phenology" in the United States.[7]

Thoreau, in his interest in relationships in nature, must concern
himself with the continual struggle for survival undergone by plants
and animals of various species. Here, he appreciates the impartiality of
science; it looks on what may be a life-and-death struggle and takes no
sides. He does not become sentimental about the vanquished but maintains a kind of scientific objectivity in witnessing their death. If the
"death of the flea and the elephant are but phenomena of the life of
nature" (VII, 324), he will see these deaths as just that—phenomena.
They are the *natural* thing. When he hears a hawk scream harshly, he
believes it to be "fitted" (X, 103) to do so in order to excite terror in its
prey and by that means detect it; and when he sees a pickerel swallowing
a struggling minnow, he realizes that both fish are fulfilling their destiny.

Thoreau describes such constituents of the world in a way that recalls
for us the old concept of the Great Chain of Being, but in his treatment
in *Walden* they come to be considered as part of the food chain which
is the study of modern-day biologists: "The perch swallows the grub-
worm, the pickerel swallows the perch, and the fisherman swallows

the pickerel; and so all the chinks in the scale of being are filled" (II, 314). A more complex analysis is given in the *Journal* (IX, 459). There is a "wonderful greediness" (XX, 331) with which each organism seems to contend for possession of the earth, he says. Then land with its predator and victim is a battlefield, a "Golgotha" (XVI, 435), and the ocean a "vast *morgue*" (IV, 186). Even his memorable description of nightfall in *Walden* which begins with the sentence—"This is a delicious evening, when the whole body is one sense, and imbibes delight through every pore"—comes at last to this statement: "The wildest animals do not repose, but seek their prey now" (II, 143).

Thoreau, it seems, imbibes his sensuous delight from the warfare of nature as well as from any other of nature's aspects. Redness in tooth and claw does not offend his senses. Nowhere is his appreciation of the harsher aspects of nature so emphasized as in *Walden*. Besides his fascination with the "heroic" battle between two kinds of ants, previously referred to, where the carnage is like an Austerlitz, we have this passage: "I love to see that Nature is so rife with life that myriads can be afforded to be sacrificed and suffered to prey on one another; that tender organizations can be so serenely squashed out of existence like pulp . . .; and that sometimes it has rained flesh and blood. . . . The impression made on a wise man is that of universal innocence" (II, 350–351). The raining of flesh and blood has its parallel in the common expression of raining cats and dogs, which he must have had in mind, and the first, he is saying, is as innocent as the latter.

Of course, Thoreau's enthusiasm here has its intellectual as well as sensuous grounds; the two are not wholly unrelated. He may see in this instance the amorality of nature and therefore the absence of evil in the struggle. Nature is simply emphasizing the present moment in the cycle of birth, decay, and death, "remembering" not that certain organisms once *were* living, but that others *are* living now. As well, he himself, we have seen, likes to live in the present, to sense the present moment, even if it involves nature's warfare. Furthermore, he knows that the struggle for survival is not only a self-assertion. It can mean too a helping of one another, a symbiosis, as in the situation which he outlines in his "Succession of Forest Trees." Also, he knows that "in Nature nothing is wasted. Every decayed leaf and twig is only better fitted to serve in some other department" (XIV, 110). His sensuous enjoyment need not be lessened.

A further matter bearing upon Thoreau's enthusiasm in this regard concerns Darwin's development theory about the struggle in nature. On January 1, 1860, Thoreau has occasion to discuss Darwin's newly published *Origin of Species*, 1859, and, liking the book, quickly secures a copy to read for himself. Already Thoreau had a previous acquaintance with the scientist, having in 1851 read the account of his voyage on the *Beagle*, the journey which gave rise to his evolutionary beliefs. Thoreau had taken eleven pages of notes on it in his *Journal* and, it would seem, respects this author who marveled at the sights and sounds of nature, as he does himself, and who stressed the interdependence of all living things.

Thoreau would also probably be predisposed to accept Darwin's later views because of the Transcendental notion of progress. In the same year that Thoreau reads of the voyage, he writes about this notion in terms of sensuous experience: "The cricket, the gurgling stream, the rushing wind amid the trees, all speak to me soberly yet encouragingly of the steady onward progress of the universe" (VIII, 391). Nature, he says in *A Week*, "has perfected herself by an eternity of practice" (I, 340). This statement (although evolutionists would modify it to read—nature *is* perfecting itself . . .), along with his idea that nature is a "careful gardener" (VIII, 265), appears to harmonize with Darwin's conviction concerning natural selection. Here would be further reason for Thoreau's acceptance of the struggle for survival in nature. In at least two journal passages he does speak against special creation and sees that the development theory implies a "sort of constant *new* creation" (XX, 147) and a "steady progress according to existing laws" (XX, 311). But Darwin's theory becomes well-known only late in his life so that it has no great influence on his overall thought. It is probably most correct to say that Thoreau's blithe feelings towards nature's warfare stem chiefly from his letting his sensuous enjoyment of the outdoor world override any qualms dictated by intellect. He states in one letter that one could mourn for every dead leaf but that it is better to smell the fragrance of autumn.

Thoreau's attitude towards the dead in nature is quite different from his attitude towards dead specimens in a museum. "I hate museums" (VII, 464), he begins a typical outburst on the subject. Scientists have no right, he feels, to make animals return, instead of to dust, to sawdust.

Yet he can appreciate the value of such collections and often visits those of the Boston Natural History Society. As well, he contributes specimens to them himself, such as a goshawk, a bird rare in that area, and on another occasion he sends Louis Agassiz of Harvard a species of mouse. It is more typical of Thoreau, however, to have a live mouse run onto his outstretched hand, as he describes in *Walden*, and then to observe its feeding habits. The proper museum is one where plants and animals live their natural lives, he tells us, "where one faint trill from a migrating sparrow [will] set the world on its legs again." A dry and dusty museum, on the other hand, has little to offer his "right-perceiving senses" and is an affront to them (VII, 464–465). The scientists there give you the body (or a facsimile) but not the bird. Its song has been lost to the sense of hearing so that, as Thoreau points out, the goose with golden eggs has been killed again. He feels himself none the wiser for knowing the length of its entrails. Using another image, this time more directly pertaining to sensuousness, he says: "Science is often like a grub which, though it may have nestled in the germ of a fruit, has merely blighted or consumed it and never really tasted it" (XVIII, 23).

Thoreau also has misgivings about the scientific names attached to specimens. He does recognize that with a knowledge of a plant or animal's name comes a "distincter recognition and knowledge of the thing" (XVII, 137). And he does see some value in the precision of scientific terms. It alone can make botany worth studying, he feels. Such is his one view. On the other hand, he feels too as Jonathan Swift did when the Brobdingnagians classified the diminutive Gulliver[8] — that scientific terms are bestowed on an object to mask our ignorance of it, and thereafter they prevent us from seeing it clearly. The technical name is but a "convenience" (XIX, 155), all right only for stating meager truths; "the most important will always be the most easy to communicate" (IX, 328).

This second view is more in accord with Thoreau's sensuous outlook, with its emphasis on the concrete, and promotes his continuing preference of an Indian's names for natural phenomena to the scientist's. "The most important part of an animal is its *anima*, its vital spirit" (XIX, 154), he says, and the Indian's acquaintance with wild nature, his having "better senses than our race" (XVI, 294), helps him to incorporate this spirit in the names which he gives to natural objects. It is that element, we know, which is of concern to Thoreau. Any names of objects, he says elsewhere, are really not of so much importance themselves compared to the exhilaration which those objects excite.

Much of Thoreau's criticism leveled at science is against the whole dry-as-dust taxonomical approach of his own day. As well as the nomenclature, the usual scientific account in itself draws his adverse comment. In believing that the truest description of an object is given by a person who is inspired by that object, he sees that the descriptions of flowers, for example, in a contemporary botany text are not written by such a person. There is much detail but little of the flowers' flower-like properties: "Not how good they are to wear on the bosom, or [their] smell, how much they are to the eye and the sentiments, not how much to the palate and the sensations" (IX, 252). When in another instance he considers a scientist's description of the stars, Thoreau's sentiments anticipate those of Walt Whitman in the poem, "When I Heard the Learn'd Astronomer."[9] Thoreau says: "nothing which the astronomers have said attaches to them, they are so simple and remote" (XIII, 60). Looking at similar reports of a scientific association, he is put off with "a parcel of dry technical terms . . . . I cannot help suspecting that the life of these learned professors has been almost as inhuman and wooden as a rain-gauge or self-registering magnetic machine" (XII, 238). Recording statistics of phenomena has its place, but where, he wants to know, is the man who would record the fairer sunsets.

"Your observation, to be interesting, *i.e.* to be significant," Thoreau writes in his *Journal*, "must be *subjective*" (XII, 237). Later, on the same page, he rephrases the notion by saying that a person must simply "tell the story of his love." The idea, we find, is often repeated in his writings. He wonders if it is possible to understand a phenomenon apart from the impression it makes, and poses this situation: "If I were to discover that a certain kind of stone by the pond-shore was affected, say partially disintegrated, by a particular natural sound, as of a bird or insect, I see that one could not be completely described without describing the other. I am that rock by the pond-side" (XV, 275). His sensuous response is a part of the total phenomenon. Poets, he feels, do describe this relationship, and his several criticisms of science, as contrasted to poetry, focuses upon this very failing to do so. The scientist coolly looks down from a mountain with his telescope while the poet standing there exults in the view. The same bald natural facts are about both, but because the poet explores the "mysterious relation between [him]self and these things" (IX, 428), he extracts the pleasure of poetry from them.

Since natural phenomena are always more to Thoreau than a scientist would make them out to be, Thoreau is really man *naturalizing* rather than a naturalist, just as he is "man writing" (VIII, 441) rather than a writer. He is a natural philosopher "to boot" (XI, 4), that is, in addition to his other pursuits. He is man first, a sensuous man in his case, who enjoys nature and wishes to know and to experience personally as much of it as possible. Such was the approach taken by the old naturalists, he tells us. They were "so sensitive and sympathetic to nature that . . . . it was an incessant miracle to them" (XIX, 180). He singles out again the early botanist John Gerard as one who had "not only heard of and seen and raised a plant but felt and smelled and tasted it, applying all his senses to it" (XX, 119). As well, Thoreau finds Audubon's writings a "thrill of delight" because the famous ornithologist sensed the whole wilderness world he was traversing. In this sense he too was "man naturalizing," having more than just a specialized interest in birds. Reading him, Thoreau finds his own senses stimulated: "I seem to hear the melting of the snow on the forks of the Missouri" (VII, 305–306). Both Gerard and Audubon had the wisdom that does not only inspect but beholds.

Many of Thoreau's own descriptions are akin to those of the old-time naturalists in his seeing the world as miraculous, as sensation-al. Two accounts, both dealing with the phenomenon of light, serve as examples. In one he is describing the northern lights (VIII, 479). He does not want to explain them in terms of electromagnetic forces but to picture the sense of grandeur they impart. He does so by using an image of Hyperborean gods burning brush — "and [the fire] spread, and all the hoes in heaven couldn't stop it." There is both awe felt, in the witnessing of gods, and, as the description continues, an excitement, from being onlooker to a runaway fire.

In the other account, described in *The Maine Woods* (III, 198–201), he sees phosphorescent wood for the first time. He starts to give a more or less scientific description, telling us the precise size of the ring of light he sees and the kind of wood in which it is found. But then he cuts some chips into his hand, and he begins to feel the wonderment of a boy with a new-found treasure, waking his companion to show them to him. "I exulted," he writes, "like 'a pagan suckled in a creed' that had never been worn at all, but was bran-new, and adequate to the occasion. I let science slide, and rejoiced in that light as if it had been a fellow creature . . . . A scientific *explanation*, as it is called, would have been altogether out of place there." It is his personal acquaintance with this phenomenon, the joy he receives from sensing it, which he wishes to describe.

Thoreau's quarrel with the science of his day is further promoted because his mind tends to see the end in the means — as we have previously noted with regard to his economics and writing. He therefore is prone to see the "means" of science — its measurements and accumulation of facts — becoming its end too — and he disapproves. To some degree he is right, the larger end having been lost sight of by the Obed Bats of his day. Making an extreme statement, he can say in 1860: "All science is only makeshift, a means to an end which is never attained" (XX, 117). This concern is with him during much of his adult life, for already in his first book eleven years earlier he has stated: "Our books of science, as they improve in accuracy, are in danger of losing the freshness and vigor and readiness to appreciate the real laws of Nature" (I, 388). He then goes on to admire Isaac Newton, whom he esteems as much as the less sophisticated old-time naturalists. Newton acted in the interests of true science, his end having been the discovery of universal laws. Such discovery to Thoreau would be a kind of knowledge of the grand rhythm of the universe with which he wishes to keep pace.

It is Newton's approach that Thoreau must have in mind as a touchstone when he later directs one of his sharpest barbs at nineteenth-century science. The great scientist and mathematician had pictured himself as a rapt child wandering along a beach, picking up a pebble or shell, while the vast ocean of truth lay undiscovered before him. Thoreau sees such attitude as a "rare mood" in contemporary science; its concern is narrowly with weighing and measuring new pebbles. "Her votaries," he says, "may be seen wandering along the shore of the ocean of truth, with their backs to that ocean . . . . You would say that the scientific bodies were terribly put to it for objects and subjects" (XVII, 359–360). The procedures of science, as they exist in his day, Thoreau finds just too limiting for his purposes as a naturalist, which involve his whole sensuous self. His sensuous approach has prompted him as we have seen, to anticipate the broader perspective of the modern scientist by his attacks on taxonomy, his strictures on available terminology, and his concern for a more comprehensive ecological overview.

Thoreau, it is true, is quite conscious of his own increasing propensity to be concerned with scientific details. He often speaks out against having an excessive concern with them—when a maiden's cheek is rosy, why bother to inquire after her diet, he asks. He fears at times, however, that "in exchange for views as wide as heaven's cope, [he is] being narrowed down to the field of the microscope" (VIII, 406). His Transcendentalism, which prompts him to see wholes rather than details, bewails this propensity while his Yankee pragmatism tells him that one must "count the cats in Zanzibar" (II, 354) until one can do better. In the later years of his life he does seem sometimes to be collecting data that he may not know quite what to do with. But there is always the chance that with enough details he may perhaps distinguish in them some universal pattern or rhythm. If not, he enjoys the exercise for its own sake. If fact will not flower into truth, he believes, as we know from his statement in the last years of his life, that "unconsidered expressions of our delight which any natural object draws from us are something complete and final in themselves" (XX, 117).

7 Hearing Beyond the Range of Sound

John Burroughs says that Thoreau collects information about nature "as the meditative saunterer gathers a leaf."[1] The term "saunterer" is a fitting description of Thoreau. Not only does he "saunter" to his task, as he affirms one should do in *A Week* (I, 110), but almost every day he walks outdoors from three to four hours. In the beginning of his essay on this activity, "Walking," he writes about the derivation of the word, "saunterer" and prefers to derive it from *Saint-Terrer*, a Holy-Lander, for such a man, he feels, is a kind of pilgrim. Thoreau's own mecca for sauntering lies westward, and he tends to begin his daily walk in that direction. To him the west, we know, speaks for wildness. In that direction is his frontier where he might enjoy an original relation to the universe,[2] the moments of most intense relationship amounting to a kind of mysticism. Sauntering physically is thus paralleled by a relaxed spiritual sauntering—the best way, he finds, to achieve moments of mystic insight.

John Macy in *The Spirit of American Literature*, 1913, often called one of the most influential books of its kind, describes two kinds of mystic: "One shrouds himself in his cloudy dreams, mistaking his murky vision for fact. The other, open-eyed and cheerful amid the sunlit world, feels himself near the heart of living things."[3] Although both descriptions appear to some extent appropriate to Thoreau, his moments of mysticism generally are those which pertain to the open-eyed kind of mystic. Then, sensuousness, visual and otherwise, is related to his visionary experiences—the means of achieving these experiences, their prevalence in his life, his attempts to compensate for their absence, and his understanding of God and the laws of the universe. His "mysticism" may be termed a super-sensuousness.

It is true that Thoreau in early manhood does say it is "with closed ears and eyes" that he "consult[s] consciousness for a moment" and "immediately are all walls and barriers dissipated." "Earth," he continues, "rolls from under me, and I float, by the impetus derived from the earth and the system, . . . in the midst of an unknown sea . . ." (VII, 53). James Russell Lowell would dismiss this kind of experience with his comment on Thoreau that being misty was not being mystic.[4] And at first glance Thoreau's approach here does seem somewhat "misty" or "murky," for the phrase, "with closed ears and eyes," begins the account. An initial steeping in sensations is not mentioned. Yet such steeping, we find, is characteristic of the mystical approach to nature of certain British Romantics with whom Thoreau is sometimes linked, particularly William Wordsworth.

With Wordsworth, sensuous perception can lead to an experience of suspended *being* — a being part of the natural world as its constituents themselves are — which in turn leads to spiritual perception. In *The Excursion*, 1814, he writes of a boy[5] holding a seashell to his ear, and by listening "intensely," he feels "mysterious union with its native sea." Such experience makes one "brightened with joy" and, Wordsworth believes, imparts "authentic tidings of invisible things."[6] M. H. Abrams points out that most frequently with the poet himself, while his senses are thus fixed on an object, they are not mastered by it — it is the object which becomes "suddenly charged with revelation."[7] In this way, "the meanest flower that blows can give / Thoughts that do often lie too deep for tears" ("Ode: Intimations of Immortality").[8] On occasion, however, sensations of nature can give such a profound feeling that the sense data themselves are forgotten in what Geoffrey H. Hartman sees as Wordsworth's "apocalyptic" attitude towards nature. Nature is obliterated as he achieves "an unmediated contact with the principle of things."[9] The situation is described in *The Prelude*, 1850, where spiritual perception of truth occurs: "the light of sense / Goes out, but with a flash that has revealed / The invisible world."[10] The truth thus gained is not only of temporary value, because the intuitive flashes can be recreated in "hours of weariness" so that the mind and heart are filled with "tranquil restoration" ("Tintern Abbey").[11]

With Thoreau, it would appear that his description of the mystic experience, in which he momentarily consults "consciousness" with *closed* ears and eyes and then floats "by the impetus derived from earth and the system," is much akin to that described in *The Excursion* (apart from the sea image to be referred to later). He has merely neglected to describe his initial stage of sensuous perception. That the "impetus" stems from "the earth and the system" suggests that the sensuous indeed is required as a starting position. Other accounts by him, we shall see in this chapter, have this Wordsworthian feature. And just as the *Excursion* passage comes to speak of a "central peace, subsisting at the heart / Of endless agitation,"[12] so the account in Thoreau's *Journal* closes with reference to a "restful kernel in the magazine of the universe" (VII, 54).

Thoreau's use of the word "consciousness" also needs to be explained, and for doing so the passage pertaining to it, already referred to, should be quoted at length (the quotation offers some similarities to that cited from *The Prelude*):

> If with closed ears and eyes I consult consciousness for a moment, immediately are all walls and barriers dissipated, earth rolls from under me, and I float, by the impetus derived from the earth and the system, a subjective heavily laden thought, in the midst of an unknown and infinite sea, or else heave and swell like a vast ocean of thought, without rock or headland, where are all riddles solved, all straight lines making their two ends meet, eternity and space gambolling familiarly through my depths. I am from the beginning, knowing no end, no aim. No sun illumines me, for I dissolve all lesser lights in my own intenser and steadier light. I am a restful kernel in the magazine of the universe. (VII, 53–54)

If the peak of his experience is a sense of *being* (as it is with Wordsworth), then what Thoreau is involved with is not so much "consciousness" as "*un*consciousness," an unconsciousness of self which is yet awareness. The light of sense has gone out (no sun illumines him), leaving an awareness of a previously invisible world where all riddles are solved. Fortunately, Thoreau in the same volume of his *Journal* provides us with a clue for interpreting his use of the term "consciousness." The statement in question has been alluded to in an earlier chapter: "The unconsciousness of man," he writes, "is the consciousness of God" (VII, 119). Then the consciousness he "consult[s]" is God's, which is the same as his own unconsciousness. Thus he becomes one with God's universe.

Thoreau's image of floating on an "unknown and infinite sea" is effective in portraying his departure from the conscious world, from the solid material world of rocks and headlands. Samuel Taylor Coleridge, in "This Lime-Tree Bower My Prison," uses the term, "swimming sense,"[13] to describe a similar state. Wordsworth, we noted, uses a like image in *The Excursion* (Thoreau would have enjoyed the pun on *"tidings* of invisible things"), and also, as Hartman states, makes a flooded world his recurring image of revelation of truth. The poet speaks of "that immortal sea / Which brought us hither," with its "mighty waters rolling evermore," in his "Ode: Intimations of Immortality."[14] The picture reminds us of the Biblical one in Genesis where the waters have been newly created, with God hovering over the face of them. The flood, then, stands for the nearness of God.[15] The sea of course is a common image of truth. Herman Melville, we know, has his narrator in *Moby-Dick,* 1851, say that the highest truth resides in outright landlessness,[16] and Thoreau himself has used the expression, "ocean of knowledge," elsewhere in the *Journal* (X, 289). Hence the ocean is the place, fittingly, where all riddles should be solved, as he claims they are in the quoted passage.

But what are the answers? Thoreau does not say. He probably would have enjoyed punning that they are in fact "solutions," that is, "dissolved" ungraspable phantoms in the ocean of truth: "I dissolve all lesser lights in my own intenser and steadier light," he writes. We, the readers, cannot be sure even what the riddles are. Instead of any being solved, it is more likely that for him they have been at best simply posed before being blotted out or "dissipated" as are the walls and barriers of the finite world. He says later in life that knowledge amounts to nothing more than "an indefinite sense of the grandeur and glory of the universe" (VIII, 168). And in *Walden* he speaks of catching a bit of stardust, of clutching a segment of rainbow—both vague phrases pertaining to the aftermath of a mystic experience. Then, although he proceeds to mystic insight in a fashion similar to Wordsworth's, he does not come back with any explicit truths, with any propositions proved true.[17] The overall experience still has its material benefit for him in that he once again, as with so much of his activity, finds the end in the means — in this case, in steeping himself in sensations, with the possibility that the experience attain the level of mysticism or the intensity of what others call mystical feeling.

Thoreau writes that the more wonderful objects he *beholds* in a day, the more "expanded and immortal" he becomes (XV, 45–46). A key word in Macy's definition of the second kind of mystic, we recall, is "open-eyed." In another description pertaining to mystical experience, Thoreau suggests that like some watchman in an ancient city, he will gladly watch open-eyed a whole year from the city's walls if he can feel himself "elevated for an instant upon Pisgah" — if "the world which was dead prose to [him] become living and divine" (VIII, 471). "Pisgah" does not really signify a wish to be shown a Promised Land (Deut. XXXIV. 1) but a wish to have a heightened response to the ordinary world, as the second part of the quotation makes clear.

At times Thoreau seems to watch his world so acutely that he actually *begins* to feel one with the phenomena he witnesses; for example, he so closely observes a fish that he begins to feel "amphibious" (VII, 120). His consciousness of the fish, which separates him from its world, gives way to his being part of that world — and yet not wholly so. He has used the word "amphibious" — rather than "piscine," which would apply strictly to the fishy world. That is, there is not a full mystic union: he has not identified himself completely with the fish but instead becomes imaginatively that amphibious creature which retains his own (terrestrial) characteristics while adding those of the fish.[18] Thoreau's heightened response, we find, can verge more into complete mysticism when in yet another account he stands "open-*eared*" to a strain of music: "No particulars survive this expansion; persons do not survive it. In the light of this strain there is no thou nor I. We are actually lifted above ourselves" (XV, 222). Music particularly, and particularly the "music" heard in the outdoor world, can have such effect on him. It lifts him up above the dust of the universe, "over the field of [his] life," and after the interval he is left with "an ectasy of joy" (XV, 217).

Like Macy's second kind of mystic again—and like Wordsworth's boy with the seashell—Thoreau, we note, is cheerful. "Surely joy is the condition of life" (V, 106), he has stated in an early essay (1842); and the excitement he ever feels in his sensuous perception of each changing aspect of nature makes him exclaim later that God could not be unkind to him if He wanted to (XV, 160). Every day is an opportunity to go to "fresh woods and pastures new" (a passage from Milton he loves to quote), the "revelations of nature" being "infinitely glorious and cheering, hinting . . . of possibilities untold" (VIII, 207). In spite of some sober moments of nostalgia, common to any man, he is aptly described by members of his family: "they could never be sad in his presence . . . ; he had been the happiest person they had ever known, all through his life."[19]

The mystic process for Thoreau, then, tends to be different from that outlined in Evelyn Underhill's monograph on the subject, *Mysticism*, 1955, in which he discusses five stages leading to a mystic union.[20] Although he says that some of the stages may be blurred or omitted, he finds that a degree of dejection or stress forms a part of several of the stages. For example, the first stage—awakening of the self—is not a sudden conversion but a sequel to prolonged uncertainty and mental stress. The second stage—purification of the self—is a feeling of self-reproach as one wishes to purge away the human instinct for personal happiness. The third stage—illumination—with its clarity of vision and joyous apprehension, does apply to Thoreau, but in Underhill's schema it gives way to the fourth stage—the "dark night of the soul." Here there is a feeling of deprivation and desertion, before the final stage—union—occurs. With Thoreau, there is no real sense of contrition, nor little oscillation between states of dark despair and sunny elation. At most there is a wavering between two attitudes, of alertness and inattention, rather than between two emotions. "Not by constraint or severity," he tells us, "shall you have access to true wisdom, but by abandonment, and childlike mirthfulness. If you would know aught, be gay before it" (VII, 150).

Thoreau's problem in attaining mystic insight is to reconcile an attitude of abandonment with one of watchfulness. For his desire, as he expresses it, to become intoxicated with the fumes of divine nectar is constant—his profession "is to be *always* on the alert to find God in nature, to know his lurking-places" (VIII, 472) [my italics]. However, he comes to realize that by striving to be constantly alert, he stays short of his goal, for he is apt to become absorbed in this very striving. He discovers that when he is abstracted enough, even the opaque earth itself reflects images to him; that is, he looks into a visionary world. He cites the example of a woodchopper who, although not given to mystical experience, is so bent on his work among the trees and not upon the impressions they are fitted to make that he "forgets himself, forgets to observe, and at night he *dreams* of [them]" [Thoreau's italics]. The chopper, according to Thoreau, has passed enough of his "unconscious life" in the woods in order to have "incommunicable knowledge" concerning them (IX, 123–124). His "dreams," if part of a waking experience, would be a kind of mysticism.

Thus, we find Thoreau himself spending many an hour lying across the seats of his boat, "dreaming awake," drifting about Walden Pond (II, 213). He describes such an incident in the *Journal* in these terms: "I almost cease to live and begin to be." "I am never so prone to lose my identity," he goes on; "I am dissolved in the haze" (VII, 75). At such time his mysticism *approaches* the Eastern variety, where the self is annihilated in union (in Western or Christian mysticism, the mystic can live in both this world and the world of the spirit simultaneously). In similar fashion Thoreau sits yogi-like in the sunny doorway of his hut for an entire day, apparently becoming absorbed in Atman or divinity through achieving the Oriental forsaking of works by contemplation. He uses language with a religious flavor to describe his timeless experience: "it was morning, and lo, now it is evening, and nothing memorable is accomplished" (II, 124).

Whatever Oriental overtones — or, as Thoreau says, a mingling of Walden water with that of the Ganges — we find in *Walden*, we should remember, however, that Thoreau like all Transcendentalists, is eclectic in accepting only those facets of Oriental philosophy which appeal to him, while ignoring the rest. In the *Bhagavad-Gita*,[21] which he speaks of reading while at the pond, Krishna — an incarnation of Brahman, the total godhead — asserts the values of solitude and of a desirelessness for material wealth. In these features Thoreau would find a philosophy of life which confirms his own. But he would not agree with Krishna's statement that a devotee does not rejoice in what is pleasant. Nor would he agree with Krishna's general denigration of the senses: Krishna says that a man is illumined when he can still the senses, for they set his better judgment adrift. Thoreau for the most part remains at the level of sensing "Brahman" in all exterior objects — and enjoys doing so. Even in the experience within the sunny doorway, he does not give way to complete abandonment, for he hears meanwhile the singing of birds, and like them he has his "chuckle or suppressed warble" (II, 124) of inner rejoicing at his good fortune.

Thoreau says at one juncture in the *Journal* that it is by forgetting yourself and your quest that you approach God (VIII, 3), but he is more specific in a letter, which also touches upon the relationship between watchfulness and abandonment: "It is not when I am going to meet [God], but when I am just turning away and leaving him alone, that I discover that God is" (VI, 178). At the point of turning away, he is in a "subdued and knocking mood" (XIX, 111) when he is most receptive to influences. In turning away, too, he sees with the unworn sides of his eye. With such perception insight may come. He describes the experience:

> I had seen into paradisaic regions . . . , and I was no longer wholly or merely a denizen of this vulgar earth. Yet had I hardly a foothold there. I was only sure that I was charmed and no mistake. It is only necessary to behold thus the least fact or phenomenon, however familiar, from a point a hair's breadth aside from our habitual path or routine, to be overcome, enchanted by its beauty and significance. (XIV, 44)

It is watchfulness *followed* by abandonment which seems to lead to moments of insight.

Thoreau admits that deliberate preparation does not necessarily bring these moments into being. They remain unbribed as the coming of dawn. He is confronted with a problem similar to one confronting the Puritan theologians concerning the advent of grace.[22] He realizes as they did that there is a paradox in somehow preparing for, willing oneself to prepare for, what can only be a passive reception. A Wordsworthian wise passiveness or, in his own terms, an "unanxious labor" (*LJ*, 167) may achieve for him that fairer morning. His account of pursuing a loon on Walden Pond might well describe the elusiveness of the mystic experience: "it was as well for me to rest on my oars and wait his reappearing as to endeavor to calculate where he would rise; for . . . when I was straining my eyes over the surface one way, I would suddenly be startled by his unearthly laugh behind me" (II, 261).

The more intense moments of mysticism — those approaching a trance-like state — seem to come more readily to Thoreau in his youth than later in his life. He shares the belief, subscribed to by Wordsworth and Henry Vaughan and dating back to Plato, that the young are closer to God than are adults. At times he specifically voices the notion that we come from a pre-existent heavenly state and that life on earth is a retreat from God. The youth, a "demigod," is "prompted by the reminiscence of that other sphere from which he so lately arrived, [and] his actions are unintelligible to his seniors" (XIX, 35). Thoreau says that a child discerns the true laws of life and relations more clearly than do adults, and he feels that he is not so wise as the day he was born. With the child the insight is an unconscious thing, even as Thoreau's early experiences seem to be: "There was a time when the beauty and the music were all within . . . . When you walked with a joy which knew not its origin. When you were an organ of which the world was but one poor broken pipe. I lay long on the rocks, foundered like a harp on the seashore, that knows not how it is dealt with" (XII, 294).

It is a common image in Romantic literature to see man as a harp, particularly an aeolian harp, played upon by the forces of nature.[23] For example, Percy Bysshe Shelley wants to be a lyre to the west wind in his famous ode;[24] Coleridge speaks of an intellectual breeze sweeping through all animated things in "The Eolian Harp."[25] There is a kind of divine breath inspiring the poet in his creation: the Latin *spiritus* signifies wind and breath, so that to be played upon harp-like by a wind, representing some vital force in nature, is to be "in-spired" in both senses of the word.[26] But Thoreau's youthful experience in which he walks "with a joy which knew not its origin" is an end in itself, having no purpose but, as he says elsewhere, "to have such sweet impressions made on us, such ecstasies begotten of the breezes!" He knows not *how* he is exactly dealt with, but he "perceives that [he] is dealt with by superior powers" (VIII, 307). He is like his own telegraph harp, which seems to carry the "sound of a far-off glorious life, a supernal life" (VIII, 450). He has had intimations of immortality, has felt the "Bright *shootes* of everlastingness" which Vaughan has spoken of in "The Retreate."[27]

Thoreau regrets the loss of these youthful experiences—"How much . . . that is best in our experience in middle life may be resolved into the memory of our youth!" (X, 460)—but he has no wish to revel in melancholy as some European Romantics tended to do. Instead, he cannot resist punning in the poem "Music" that he has lost his *boy*ant step. And in *Walden* he (as the hermit) writes of the trance-like state in jocular fashion:

> I was as near being resolved into the essence of things as ever I was in my life. I fear my thoughts will not come back to me. If it would do any good, I would whistle for them . . . . What was it I was thinking of? It was a very hazy day. I will just try these three sentences of Confut-see; they may fetch that state again. I know not whether it was the dumps or budding ecstasy. (II, 269)

Several other passages reveal that Thoreau's sometime regret about losing his youth concerns a matter particularly applicable to him individually. Here is one such passage, which bears a close examination:

> I think that no experience which I have to-day [1851] comes up to, or is comparable with, the experiences of my boyhood. And not only this is true, but as far back as I can remember I have unconsciously referred to the experiences of a previous state of existence. "For life is a forgetting" etc. . . . My life was ecstasy. In youth, before I lost any of my senses, I can remember that I was alive . . . . (VIII, 306)

In the first sentence of the quotation, Thoreau is simply stating a feeling most people have in looking back on their lives: to say that no days seem as good as those of childhood and youth is a commonplace. The next few sentences voice the sentiments of Wordsworth's "Ode: Intimations of Immortality from Recollections of Early Childhood," but whether Thoreau is overly occupied with this notion is doubtful. His many attestations throughout his writings are about the importance of the present world, as Chapter 1 has earlier indicated. Indeed, if he can criticize Christianity for emphasizing another (future) world when his senses tell him that this world is heaven enough, then his criticisms might also be directed at those who extol another (past) world from which we supposedly trail clouds of glory. His brief quotation from Wordsworth, quoted incorrectly[28] and *followed by* "etc.," could be interpreted as revealing his impatience to get on to another notion. Now, it seems, he comes at last to say what *he* feels to be important: "In youth, *before I lost any of my senses . . .*" [my italics]. What he regrets with his increasing age is the dulling of his own sense perception, his approach to nature being a sensuous one. Other entries in his *Journal* corroborate this view. "The senses of children are unprofaned. Their whole body is one sense" (VIII, 291), he writes in 1851. Two years later he writes: "Ah, those youthful days! are they never to return? when the walker does not too curiously observe particulars, but sees, hears, scents, tastes, and feels only himself, — the phenomena that show themselves in him" (XI, 75).

If the moments of budding ecstasy gradually become fewer for Thoreau, they are replaced by moments also satisfying in his relationship to nature. In his long — call it — marriage to nature, his early fervor becomes tempered and mellowed. The heady wine of the marriage feast of Cana gives way to a less intoxicating but richer wine. The best wine, after all, of any marriage comes toward the end and is something which must be striven for. In his poem "Manhood" he gives preference over the child to the adult who "has proudly steered his life with his own hands."[29] As Thoreau grows older, he consciously seeks communion with nature; he no longer relies on an unconscious intercourse with it. He must keep the aeolian harp that he is, in harmony with nature's forces, "continually trying its strings to see if they are in tune" (XI, 424). By keeping his senses crystalline, he can still hope to be inspired in some manner, to have deep-blue water, for instance, "blue" (XII, 165) his soul again. He had been doubting, he writes in 1854, if the song of the thrush would still affect him as of yore, but, he can add, "it [does] measurably" (XII, 225).

Thoreau continues his daily walks, filled with hope and faith, or rather, with his hope becoming his faith. Will not this frame of mind "make to itself ears at length" (VII, 321) with which to hear celestial sounds, he has earlier asked. He in effect, is striving for a super-sensuousness. "Our present senses," he tells us, "are but the rudiments of what they are destined to become. We are comparatively deaf and dumb and blind, and without smell or taste or feeling" (I, 408). He nurtures his own senses past a rudimentary stage. He already describes one of his early mystic experiences as a hearing "beyond the range of sound," a seeing "beyond the verge of sight" (I, 182). And according to a journal passage in 1853 such perception is accomplished through the physical senses. He speaks of walking out one winter evening, wishing to hear the silence of the night. He must uncover his ears to do so and then reports: "I hark the goddess Diana. The silence rings; it is musical and thrills me. A night in which the silence was audible. I hear the unspeakable" (X, 471–472).

Thoreau can hear on earth things of the heavens because, as he says in *A Week*, "here or nowhere is our heaven" (I, 405): he can conceive of nothing fairer than what he himself is capable of experiencing sensuously. He repeats this notion in *Walden* where he says that "Heaven is under our feet as well as over our heads" (II, 313), and he expands upon the idea to say that we can rise heavenward by rooting ourselves in the earth, just as a tree does. But even such rising is only *towards* heaven, as it is with Robert Frost in "Birches."[30] It is a temporary thing and we should be set down again, for earth, after all, is the right place for love. We need to be "earth-born," says Thoreau, as well as "heaven-born" (I, 405). Thus, he reiterates, "we need pray for no higher heaven than the pure senses can furnish" (I, 408).

A reliance upon pure senses could suggest a life of glad animal movements as practiced by a child. For Thoreau, however, we know that these senses are to be obtained through as conscious a refinement of their use as can be practiced by an adult. Just as Thoreau recognizes that there is a distinct animal health and vigor which when disciplined enables man to flow on an open channel of purity to God (II, 242–243), so he knows that "there are certain things which only senses refined and purified may take cognizance of" (*LJ*, 125). It is this kind of "chastity" which can lead to an "acquaintance with the All" (XV, 346): heaven is in the condition of the hearer (X, 219). The "silence," which was referred to earlier and which Thoreau capitalizes in *A Week*, is one of his terms for the celestial music or divinity which may be heard. All sounds—that is, the ordinary sounds of nature—are its servants, he tells us, and proclaim its wonders to us. "Through [Silence] all revelations have been made" (I, 419). The only sin, he notes in a letter, is to shut our ears to God's "immediate" voice (C, 52).

A man with super-senses, Thoreau implies, can hear God. Thoreau apparently not only can hear God at intervals but also can "see, smell, taste, . . . feel that everlasting Something" (I, 182); God culminates in the present moment and is to be apprehended by the "divine germs called the senses" (I, 408). Thoreau's reference to "Something" suggests his somewhat indefinite concept of deity, which needs to be considered at this time in light of his "mysticism." In this instance he expands upon "Something" to mean that "to which we are allied, at once our maker, our abode, our destiny, our very Selves" (I, 182). This concept is that of the Transcendental Oversoul, and he uses the term, "Universal Soul" (I, 131) in *A Week*. Elsewhere, however, he speaks of God as something distinct from man, but even here he is not consistent. As he stands over an insect in *Walden*, he is "reminded of the greater Benefactor and *Intelligence* that stands over [him] the human insect" (II, 365); he also says, in the *Lost Journal*, "I do not talk to any *intellect* in nature, but am presuming an infinite heart somewhere" (*LJ*, 196) [both italics mine].

Nor is Thoreau consistent in what he considers to be the relationship between God and nature. When he says that "there is suggested something superior to any particle of matter, in the idea or mind which uses and arranges the particles" (XVII, 204), he implies that God is a force external to nature. Such a deistic notion is apparent in his references to God as "Maker" (II, 214), nature being His art (I, 339); or as a shaper of mountains who, with "the plan of the universe" in mind, molded their opposite slopes to balance one another (V, 148). But his God is not just the originator of the universe and the laws by which it operates—as a clockmaker, for instance, is of a watch.[31] His God does not stand aside from His creation in a disinterested manner once it is made but takes a present "interest in the stacking of hay, the foddering of cattle, and the draining of peat meadows" (VII, 341). Sound senses, he tells us, teach us that there is a "nature" behind the ordinary (I, 409), and when he *hears* a tree fall in the woods, he concludes that a "deliberate" force overthrew it (III, 115). "If Nature is our mother," he asks on another occasion, "is not God much more?" (VII, 326). He is implying that God is a warm, protective being.

Thoreau, we see further, may be implying that God is not external to nature but that He encompasses it, that it is a part of Him. In saying elsewhere that a rainbow is a vision of God's face or that the moon is a manifestation of divinity, he indeed suggests that God dwells within nature. "God exhibits himself . . . in a frosted bush to-day, as much as in a burning one to Moses of old" (X, 443). Movements everywhere in nature such as the running of streams and the waving of trees, he feels, must surely be the circulations of God. This notion of immanence is Thoreau's prevalent position, we find, and in *A Week* he chooses to change the wording of "The Lord's Prayer," thus speaking of our Father who dwells in *earth* (I, 408). He goes so far in that book that he asks — "Is not Nature, rightly read, that of which she is commonly taken to be the symbol merely?" (I, 408). That is, nature itself may be God.

Another statement which seems to point to this conclusion is found in "Walking," where Thoreau says: "Nature is a personality so vast and universal that we have never seen one of her features" (V, 242). Since he knows his Bible well, this quotation appears to be an echo of St. Paul's epistle to the Corinthians in which the apostle compares what our knowledge of God is on earth with what it will be in the next life. He writes: "For now we see through a glass, darkly; but then face to face . . ." (I Cor. XIII. 12). Thoreau here may be equating God with nature, for he apparently paraphrases the apostle's speech about God and uses it to refer to nature. Concordantly, the rainbow mentioned previously, which is glimpsed in this life, is but a *vision* of God's face.

The notion that nature is God would make Thoreau a pantheist, but further consideration of the evidence for thinking so is not conclusive. The term "pantheism" stems from the Greek root for "all" and means that God is all of nature. The proper name of the Greek god, Pan, also has the same derivation; and from the association of his name with "all," he came to be known as an impersonation of nature — or as that deity representing all of nature. A worshipper of Pan, then, might well be a pantheist. Now, in *A Week*, Thoreau says that of all the gods, he, Thoreau, is perhaps most constant at Pan's shrine (I, 65), and in *Walden* he refers to visits from an "old settler and original proprietor" (II, 152), who most likely is Pan.[32] However, it may be that Thoreau in these instances is thinking as much of the specific Greek rural deity as he is of the impersonation of nature which Pan was later considered to be. Thoreau does give a precise description in *A Week*, referring to the god's ruddy face and shaggy body, to the pipes and crook he carries, and to his nymph and daughter; while the picture presented in *Walden* is that of an entertaining personality, given to social mirth and a pleasant view of things. Thoreau seems to have in mind a distinct personage even if it can also be a personification.

Whether or not, then, Thoreau's references to Pan make him an actual pantheist is questionable. To hold such a position exclusively would be to deny the transcendence of God, a position contrary to statements of his we have already considered. He does say at one place that he is "born to be a pantheist" but then adds "if that be the name of me" (*C*, 294). He would be more accurate if he called himself a pan*en*theist, someone who conceives of God as both immanent *and* transcendent. But it is likely that Thoreau would again attach the proviso—"if that be the name of me." He simply is not interested in theologizing about God but in experiencing God.[33] "What is religion?" he asks, and answers, "That which is never spoken" (XVII, 113). Quarreling about God is no more his propensity than quarreling with God.[34] His senses tell him that deity is everywhere apparent in nature—in an otter's tracks across a snowy landscape to the snowy landscape itself. Such evidence satisfies him. He stands in wonder before it, exhilarated because of his sensuous response:

> Why do the vast snow plains give us pleasure, the twilight of the bent and half-buried woods? Is not all there consonant with virture, justice, purity, courage, magnanimity? Are we not cheered by the sight? And does not all this amount to the track of a higher life than the otter's, a life which has not gone by and left a footprint merely, but is there with its beauty, its music, its perfume, its sweetness, to exhilarate and recreate us? (XII, 43)

The landscape, Thoreau writes in *A Week*, is "indeed something real, and solid, and sincere, and I have not put my foot through it yet"

(I, 374). Later he says that an impenetrable nature is the kind he longs for (XI, 293). While he is concerned with discovering the laws by which God operates, the laws underlying this landscape, underlying nature, he is in no haste to do so. He will rather see clearly, he tells us, a particular instance of them: "Better that the primrose by the river's brim be a yellow primrose, and nothing more, than that it be something less" (I, 111–112).[35] Nature preaches not abstract but practical truth, he says on another occasion; it does not wait to be explained. Still, he speculates in *Walden* that "if we knew all the laws of Nature, we should need only one fact, or the description of one phenomenon, to infer all the particular results at that point" (II, 320).

According to *Walden* too, Thoreau's daily intercourse with nature has gained for him some knowledge apparently of these laws as they relate to the human world. "The laws of the universe," he tells us, "are not indifferent" (II, 242). In the *Journal* he says that they are on the side of the most sensitive and tender (XI, 294). Is he here suggesting that nature itself is moral? He does seem to hear a reproof in every zephyr concerning our conduct. And he imagines that the moral laws today were natural science in some past golden age; the people then lived according to the laws of nature and made them their moral code — thus the natural laws are the "purest" morality (I, 387). They manifest themselves in beauty — every drop of rain is a rainbow from the right point of view (XIV, 45) — and in happiness — all natural objects because of their very color and form suggest "an everlasting and thorough satisfaction" (XV, 207) — and to these sensate qualities man can respond.

Thoreau also seems, at times, to feel that morality is separate from nature. It is amoral, taking no sides, being "neither radical nor conservative." "Consider the moonlight," he says, "so civil, yet so savage!" (V, 332). It may be that nature has an appearance of being a moral force for only the reason that in its varied seasons it is capable of being both a "serene friend" and a "stormy friend" (C, 38). Thoreau states his position here in these definite terms, with a comment as well on the sensuous life: "The moral aspect of nature is a jaundice reflected from man . . . . Occasionally we rise above the necessity of virtue into an unchangeable morning light, in which we have not to choose in a dilemma between right and wrong, but simply to live right on and breathe the circumambient air. There is no name for this life unless it be the very vitality of *vita*" (VII, 265). In keeping with such insight, he can reflect that lightning, for example, appeared to be a manifestation of vengeance or justice to the ancients. It was Jove's bolt, which punished the guilty. If we too entertain a similar belief, he continues, it is probably our consciousness of sin which prompts the belief. Yet later in the very same journal entry, he wonders if men are not nearer to truth with their superstitions than with their science: "Science assumes to show *why* the lightning strikes a tree, but it does not show us the moral *why* any better than our instincts did" (X, 157). That is, he seems to suggest that lightning may indeed be a moral force.

One can conclude only that Thoreau does not appear to work out a definite position on the relationship between nature and morality—and does not consider it one of his priorities to do so. His "mysticism" provides him with no outright conclusion, and he is content to say, as he does in *Walden*, that the workings of nature are "unfathomable by us because unfathomable" (II, 350). What is important to him is not so much to see a distant and visionary world where moral *why's* are explained but rather to live in *this* world be it good or bad (IV, 368). Steeped in its sensations, he can, with his "unanxious labor" and/or disciplined perception, see things in the present world as divine. Like the artist of the city of Kouroo, he would create an exemplary private world of "full and fair proportions" (II, 360) for himself out of the material and concrete. Doing so would be to escape the illusion of time, as in a mystical experience, and to rise into that "unchangeable morning light" above "the necessity of virtue." "Simply to live on" would mean to continue his sensuous approach to nature (and to its underlying laws and the God immanent within it) (VII, 265). His love of the "real, and solid, and sincere" (I, 374) landscape throughout his lifetime would prompt him to say—as he does on his deathbed concerning the next world—"One world at a time."[36] Just as his concern with God is to experience Him, as has been discussed earlier, so his concern with nature and its laws (amoral or otherwise) is similarly to experience that nature. He can take joy in the means here, the means which can, as we have seen elsewhere, become once more an end in itself.

8 The Answered Question

If in his youth Thoreau comes back with no explicit truths from these states which Norman Foerster has called moments of "sensuous dissolving into nature,"[1] the experience itself bespeaks the kinship and unity he feels does exist in all of nature and usually feels does exist between nature and man, particularly himself. In later years, as in previous ones, his crystalline senses still seem to perceive beyond those characteristics which distinguish one natural phenomenon from another and detect the underlying unity. His perception prompts him to speculate on man's place in nature and his significance there.

Thoreau readily sees a general unity in the cyclical processes of nature, in its different times of day and of year. The day, he says in *Walden*, is the epitome of the year, and in the *Journal* he gives us a concrete illustration by stating that the red sunset sky is October and the later twilight November (XVII, 243). To him, the whole year is but a single season, a spring-summer time. He senses this notion in autumn, lying on his back with joy under the boughs of a witch hazel which is blossoming while its leaves are falling. And in winter he feels that snow is "summer's canopy" (VII, 63), that the cold is merely superficial, an embellishment of summer. Far, far within, it is still summer at the core (XIII, 112). We are all hunters, he states, "pursuing the summer on snow-shoes and skates, all winter long" (XV, 164). We can appreciate his notion because of a visceral response — the correspondence of this one warm season to the vital heat which our own bodies struggle to maintain consistently through our lives. There is only one "season" too within our bodily make-up, a concept Thoreau deals with in the "Economy" chapter of *Walden*.

Thoreau's sense of doubleness helps him to see unity. Being, as he says, Indra in the sky, he can take a timeless overview, and in becoming driftwood in the stream, he attains the necessary intimacy with the natural world to sense the basic unity of its elements. Thus he senses unity in each of the animal, plant, and inanimate worlds. But he is not so successful as before in convincing us of the truth of his observations in this instance, however true they may be. During mystic moments when he takes a godlike view of creation, he may have *feelings* of there being an underlying unity, but these feelings are not translated into specific terms relating to the material world, as we have seen in the previous chapter. And the illustrations he uses now from this world seem to point to parallels but really not to concrete relationships.

For example: Thoreau sees insects, amphibians, and fish all as birds. Crickets are the very smallest of birds; frogs are birds of the night; and individual species of fish have their avian counterparts — a bream, nesting anywhere, is the homely sparrow, he tells us. In the plant world meanwhile, he sees flowers as colored leaves, and fruits as ripe ones. Such metaphors as these seem to be chiefly a part of a vivid literary technique, making us visualize the constituents of nature more precisely. So it is when he refers to inanimate things: he sees the colors of a clam's hard shell as the sky's rainbow tints extracted from the mud of a river bottom — another striking image. The saturated bottom at the same time becomes a connecting link between land and water — a "land" which has ripples, a "water" upon which one can walk. Since he notices too that the water's ripples cast their shadows on the bottom just as clouds in the sky cast shadows on the water, he says that the water is also intermediate — the intermediate liquid between solid land and airy sky.

There is kinship, Thoreau's senses tell him, among all three worlds of nature — animal, vegetable, and mineral. "How numerous the resemblances of the animate to the inanimate!" (XII, 62) he writes, and resemblances bespeak kinship to him. A violet is a part of heaven that one can smell; pickerel are "animalized *nuclei* . . . of Walden water, ... themselves small Waldens in the animal kingdom" (II, 315). Of course, he is right biologically. A plant absorbing atmosphere in its photosynthetic process of growth has transformed some of the heavens into its vegetable make-up; a fish has a similar relationship with its watery element. He is more explicit of the nature of such "unity" in describing a deer. It has a "tree" growing out of its head, indicating a "certain vegetable force . . . in the wearer" (IX, 306) and allying it to that kingdom. A further illustration becomes highly imaginative when he sees kinship between a bird and a tree. The hawk which now soars over the wood, he suggests in *A Week*, "was at first, perchance, only a leaf which fluttered in its aisles" (I, 167). In *Walden* he equates this bird not only with leaves in the wind but with ripples on the pond: "such kindredship is in nature. The hawk is aerial brother of the wave" (II, 176). Elsewhere he actually mistakes the creaking of a tree for the bird's scream.

What Thoreau appears to be aware of with all his senses are "natural rhymes, when some animal form, color, or odor has its counterpart in some vegetable" (—or mineral, one could add) (V, 127). His concept embraces the whole universe when he says that a cloud is a flower of the sky (XVI, 415) and, as well, that the heavens and earth are themselves one flower, the earth being the calyx, the heavens the corolla (XI, 225). If his literary images in this regard do not convince us of an underlying kinship, their repeated occurrence should at least serve to convince us of his own firm belief. To him, rivers, for instance, are everywhere—in trees whose currents of woody fibers and sap empty into the earth, in rivers of ore in the bowels of that earth, in stars overhead that mark the Milky Way, even in flocks of small birds which flow over a fence "as if they were not only animated by one spirit but actually held together by some invisible fluid" (VIII, 63). "Nature is one and continuous everywhere" (I, 372), he says. His statement is one with which modern science can only agree—as follows: "The web of being is in a universal seamlessness."[2]

Thoreau's conscious observations, and other sensuous responses, tell him of his own personal link to the natural world even though the unwilled mystic moments are fewer. This kinship he feels to exist despite his awareness, as he informs us in *Walden*, that the pond there has not acquired one permanent ripple through the years, while all the changes are in him. But the very structure of the same book, with its cycle of the seasons, bespeaks the relationship between himself and nature and points to the renewal of both. After a period of growth and harvest—he too growing like corn in the night—winter comes, the pond freezes over, and he withdraws inwardly, having good opportunity now to plumb the depths of his being and of the pond. Then comes the release of spring, as recorded in his exultant description in Chapter 7: all the earth is burgeoning — all is made new.

Here, Thoreau attempts with an ebullient prose style — typically with frequent exclamations — to secure for us, his readers, the emotional involvement with nature that he himself feels. In one paragraph, for example, he stumbles over words when apostrophizing a robin in order to express the excitement he shares with the creatures of spring: "O the evening robin, at the end of a New England day! If I could ever find the twig he sits upon! I mean *he*; I mean *the twig*" (II, 344). "Walden is dead and is alive again," Thoreau exclaims (II, 344) as he feels, and makes us feel through our knowledge of the Bible, the rejoicing of a father for the return of a prodigal son. But in our rejoicing, Thoreau has given us to believe, by the context in which he uses the Biblical reference, that it is nature who is our kin. Like Walden, we too can feel reborn as we give our ear to the first sparrow of the season, the twittering of martins, and the "groping clangor" (II, 345) of a goose. Thoreau is purified as if by the green flames (of grass) that he sees springing up on the hillsides. He has recovered something of the "innocence of infancy" (II, 347) by being sensuously alive to the world around him at the pond, and he has made us responsive to this world too.

Thoreau continues to feel a kinship throughout his life not only to the seasonal cycle but to all worlds of nature, animate and inanimate, just as, we already noted, he feels a kinship to exist among the constituents of those worlds. This is revealed by several journal entries in spite of his one statement in 1852 that he was once part of nature, now is merely observant of it. The year 1855 finds him flapping his elbows and crying *mow-ack* "with a nasal twang and a twist in [his] head" (XIII, 258), hoping to draw a goose down from the sky because of their kindred spirits. Camping in the Maine woods in 1857, he notices that the sound of his breathing when he is half asleep exactly resembles a loon's long-drawn call. The resemblance, he says, suggests his affinity to that bird. This last instance may simply illustrate his accepting as evidence that which he is already predisposed to believe true. But his willingness to adopt a ludicrous pose in his efforts to call a goose suggests that his belief is firmly held.

Thoreau's affinity to another class of animals, that of fish, has previously been discussed in Chapters 5 and 6, but what should be emphasized here is his consciousness that his body derives its genesis from their watery element. When he walks along the ocean, it occurs to him that man is a "product of sea-slime" (IV, 186), and thus Thoreau is linked with the cold-blooded creatures. He makes no reference to, if indeed he has knowledge of, foetal gill slits in man's neck, nor the fish's ability in emergency to gulp air into its air bladder as though it has lungs like man. Rather, we know, he has heard fish splash the surface of Walden Pond, has felt them nibble the fingers of his outstretched hand, has gazed at them asleep in their quiet parlors as though he were watching the slumber of a child or loved one: his feeling of kinship takes on a special poignancy.

Thoreau is even more closely linked with those warm-blooded creatures whose distant ancestors, an evolutionist would tell him, crept out of the slime to assume terrestrial lives. Thoreau feels a brotherhood with animals such as the fox, muskrat, and lowly skunk. What he *senses* to be true has now the backing of science. Camping along the Concord River, he hears foxes trotting about him over dead leaves, and asks: "Why should we not cultivate neighborly relations with [them]?" (VII, 89) They are "rudimental, burrowing men" (II, 301), he tells us elsewhere. He also hears a muskrat fumbling about the potatoes and melons in his boat, and the animal's presumption that the food is part of a community of goods kindles in Thoreau a "brotherly feeling" (VII, 90). If he can respect the skunk "as a human being in a very humble sphere" (XII, 162), it is not hard for him to believe as well that "even musquash are immortal" (XVII, 423).

Thoreau's feeling of kinship, however, is really not so much a matter of his elevating the animals to a human level as his being aware that he shares with them a kind of primal intelligence which is sensorimotor in nature. An animal's function is to *be*: to sense life, be influenced by it, and respond to it. The animal to a great extent smells its way through life, feels its way, finds its way by taste, sound, and sight. Although Thoreau, as man, passes beyond *being* to a position where he can perceive being and comment upon it, as a sensuous man he is particularly sensitive to the animal mode of life. As he gives chase to a fox or corners a woodchuck, incidents considered in earlier chapters, he tries to enter into these animals' worlds. He writes: "I would share every creature's suffering for the sake of its experience and joy" (IX, 367). This experience and joy, we know, can only be in terms of sensations.

Thoreau also notes his relationship to the plant world. He devotes four pages of the *Journal* (VIII, 201–205), with the help of Gray's botany manual, to drawing an analogy between human life and that of the vegetable. The comparisons, however, are fairly conventional, and the account becomes something of a mere exercise. His belief in kinship is more apparent in some shorter statements which speak of his sympathetic identification with plants. They strike us as spontaneous and as representing a true feeling. In one instance he refers to a fungus — "so obviously organic and related to ourselves" (XVII, 204). In another he asks: "Am I not partly leaves and vegetable mould myself?" (II, 153). He shares sensations with the plants. When he feels the warm sun shine on him as it also does on the St. John's-wort and life-everlasting, he believes he has some notion about the "thoughts" of these plants, for he too "lie[s] out indistinct as a heath at noonday, . . . evaporating and ascending into the sun" (VII, 203–204). His skin absorbs the warm rays so that in an autumn he feels "like a melon or other fruit laid in the sun to ripen," growing "not gray, but yellow" (XX, 73); and he says in a poem that he is "all sere and yellow" like the autumn woods themselves (I, 404).

Thoreau's principal feeling of kindredship concerning the plant world is with trees, probably partly because their firm grip on the earth aids their stately rise into the heavens — a model for the sensuous (and super-sensuous) man to emulate. And a tree, unlike most plants, lives through many cycles of the seasons, continuously experiencing winds and rains, sunshine and frost, and manifesting these "sensations" in its make-up. Thoreau says he too experiences at times the "joy" like that with which a tree buds and blossoms and reflects green rays (*LJ*, 187). When he unthinkingly casts a stone at a tree to shake down nuts, he is affected as if he had thrown the object at a "sentient being, — with a duller sense than [his] own, it is true, but yet a distant relation" (XIII, 515).

Two of Thoreau's accounts of pine trees particularly delineate his feeling of kinship. In the first one, in the *Journal* for 1851 (IX, 162–164), he describes the death of a 200-year-old tree. As the tree "fans the hillside with its fall," he describes it as a warrior "folding its mantle about it" and "embrac[ing] the earth with silent joy, returning its elements to dust again." It is a kind of funeral oration that he is giving, and he is trying to engage our sympathies, to awaken a sense of kinship in us, through this treatment. In the "Chesuncook" chapter of *The Maine Woods*, he places great emphasis on the notion that it is the *living* pine that is his kin (III, 134–135). His technique here is largely declaratory, and the trenchant tone of some of his remarks points to the vigor with which he holds his belief. A visual sensation of the trees growing in their natural state — "the tops of the pines waving and reflecting the light at a distance high over all the rest of the forest" — makes him fully realize that "a pine cut down, a dead pine, is no more a pine than a dead human carcass is a man." He affirms that every "creature" is better alive than dead, including pine trees, and that it is the living spirit of the pine with which he sympathizes. He concludes the account with a sentence which James Russell Lowell found offensive when the chapter was originally submitted to *Atlantic Monthly* and which Lowell, as editor, deleted when the essay was printed in 1858. Thoreau states his ultimate feeling of kinship with the pine in these words: "It is as immortal as I am, and perchance will go to as high a heaven, there to tower above me still."

Thoreau also feels an affinity with the non-living world, that part which never was alive. It may be that in a larger sense he believes the earth to be "all alive and covered with papillae" (II, 333). This he says in *Walden*, where the frozen pond, being sensitive to the weather, booms. He likes to think himself affected similarly: in spring the frost comes out of him, he says, and he is "heaved like the road" (XI, 34). His affinity becomes Whitmanesque in the following apostrophe where he sees the earth as the stuff of his being: "Of thee, O earth are my bone and sinew made; to thee, O sun, am I brother" (IX, 95). The "mould and mist" of earth and sky are in him, Alcott has said.[3] And if the sun is his brother, the stars can be his fellows (VII, 339).

What we are really seeing with Thoreau is a kinship of two kinds. One, he feels related because he sees that his bodily composition and its response to stimuli is analogous to that of other constituents of the world. Two, he feels related because he senses in this world a sort of familial connection, characteristic of humankind, and he too is a member, a fellow "creature" to these constituents. When he speaks elsewhere of the earth as being a mother, he is not just repeating a commonplace. He has observed—and smelled— a young turtle emerging from its egg buried in this earth. The earth has "nurse[d]" the egg, been "genial" to it. The phenomenon suggests a "certain vitality and intelligence in the earth, which [he] had not realized. This mother is not merely inanimate and inorganic" (XIII, 28). Always his keen sensuous response is important in helping him feel a kinship—as the opening sentences of the "Solitude" chapter of *Walden* make clear: it is when "the whole body is one sense" that he "go[es] and come[s] with a strange liberty in Nature, a part of herself" (II, 143). Perhaps his feeling of kinship with the universe is nowhere more convincing and better expressed than in this book when he observes the patterns which thawing earth assumes in flowing down a cutbank, previously discussed in Chapter 5. He finds that feathers, ice crystals, along with thawing clay—and man is "but a mass of thawing clay" (II, 339)—all exhibit a leaf design. All are related; nothing is inorganic.

If Thoreau is assured of man's kinship to nature, he is not so definite abut man's *place* in nature. Is nature a plant, man's abode in it a gall (caused by God's sting), and man the inner grub "completely changing the destiny of the plant," which "devotes itself to the service of the insect"—as he suggests in one passage of the *Journal* (XI, 349)? Or is man, with the "white [snow-covered] earth beneath and that spot[less] skimmed-milk sky above him, . . . but a black speck inclosed in a white egg-shell" (XVII, 445)? Thoreau would fain see a universe, he tells us in another journal passage, where man is indeed but a grain of sand. As for himself personally, according to the poem "Nature," he does not want to be the highest member in nature's choir but is satisfied to be only the breeze that blows among the reeds. Elsewhere he states that he feels complimented if nature but allows him to carry its burrs and cockles. In either case he would be sensuously involved— specifically with sound and touch in these two instances.

Thoreau knows that no matter what his situation is, he will always be the center of the world which his senses reveal to him. His position cannot be otherwise: "Let us wander where we will, the universe is built around us, and we are central still. . . . The sky is curved downward to the earth in the horizon, because I stand in the plain. I draw down the skirts. The stars so low there seem loth to go away from me, but by a circuitous path to be remembering and returning to me" (VII, 274). Similarly, looking at a sunset sky, he knows that he "always stands fronting the middle of the arch" (VIII, 296).

In this respect every man is a center of the universe, but how significant is man in the scheme of nature? Thoreau does notice a halo of light around his own shadow and therefore could think himself one of the elect (II, 224). He is like Walt Whitman in "Crossing Brooklyn Ferry" where the poet has "centrifugal spokes of light round the shape of [his] head in the sunlit water,"[4] the unusual radiance seeming to emanate from within, for it is termed "centrifugal." The appearance may be caused in part by the wheel of the ferry, which would also have spokes. Thoreau's halo too can have its scientific explanation, Thoreau himself offering one — the presence of dew on the grass. Yet he asks, as though his feeling of significance were none the less for the explanation: "Are they not indeed distinguished who are conscious that they are regarded at all?" (II, 225).

Both Whitman and Thoreau seem to be standing not only at the center of a halo of light but at the still center of the wheel of time, which is ever rushing on. Whitman says: "Just as you stand and lean on the rail, yet hurry with the swift current, I stood yet was hurried."[5] The wheel shape of the halo, and of the setting sun which makes the reflection possible for him, suggests the cyclic process of time — the sun indeed creates the diurnal and seasonal cycles — and the term "crossing," as it appears in the poem's title, suggests an eternal present, a still center of time's turning wheel. We find Thoreau too leaning on a rail in a related passage in his *Journal* (XVII, 273–274). As he waits there in the twilight, he recognizes that this (November) evening is "a familiar thing come round again." He sees himself as the spectator at the center of a painted "panorama" or cyclorama of nature in which the seasonal scenery moves around him on a continuous roll. He thinks himself "no nearer, . . . nor further off," from the moving circumference than he was the previous November; yet he is "unwilling to exchange the familiar vision that was to be unrolled for any treasure or heaven that could be imagined." As a sensuous man, he is "prepared to be pleased" again with the sight of a dark bank of clouds in the west and the song of an occasional cricket. But he does acknowledge the possibility of there being a slight change in himself between revolutions so that with added enjoyment he may extract some "new sweet" from the panorama before him.

Ever-present nature provides the environment, in a Wordsworthian sense, which can nurture in one living close to it, such as the central perceiver, a present state of happiness. This individual is like the child Thoreau speaks of who has "the wonders of nature for its toys" and so is "cherished" (VIII, 117). (One is reminded here of Wordsworth's Lucy poem, "Three Years She Grew in Sun and Shower."[6]) But, says Thoreau, "with our senses applied to the surrounding world we are reading our own physical . . . revolutions" (X, 126). Nature here would seem to be akin to man in being a kind of mirror for him. Such is the case when Thoreau one spring refers to the earth, spread out map-like around him, as the lining of his soul (XII, 294). He says this somewhat in disappointment, for again this season he is witnessing a sucker floating dead on the river. The dead fish is really within him, he claims—he is "guilty of suckers"—when what he longs for instead is "a fauna more infinite and various, birds of more dazzling colors and more celestial song." He must leave off thinking of suckers "to look at flowers and listen to birds" which match in sensuous appeal that which he has in mind. Viewing nature "humanly" (X, 163), we discover, is his concern again in his poem, "The Inward Morning," where he states that the horizon of his own mind becoming illuminated is paralleled by the hues of dawn streaking the eastern skies. It is his "inward morning" which actually institutes the day.

Man's significance seems assured. A sensuous exploration of nature in these instances for Thoreau has meant being the Lewis and Clarke of his own oceans and streams, as he says in *Walden*. He has been following the dictum of Greek philosophy—"Know thyself"—and at the end of the book he states his own version—"Explore thyself" (II, 354). Exploring thyself as the ultimate goal, that is, the emphasizing of man himself, causes the Sphinx to dash her head against a stone a second time (II, 354), for her riddle has been solved once more with an answer equivalent to the one Oedipus originally gave.[7] Thus in *Walden* Thoreau can speak of measuring the depths of one's own nature by looking into a lake. He sounds the waters of Walden Pond and finds at its bottom, even in winter, a "bright green weed" (II, 199), denoting its perennial life, and we are reminded of his description elsewhere of his soul as being a "bright invisible green" (I, 250). The coves meanwhile, their being partially landlocked or open, can tell him something about the "storms, tides, or currents" (II, 321) in his own life.

Nature can serve not only as a personal reflection to assist in gaining self-knowledge but at the same time, we find, as a symbol in verbalizing this knowledge as well. Thoreau uses part of the world as symbol to express his thought, he tells us in the *Journal* (X, 410), and in *Walden* he says he is thankful that the pond serves this purpose. With either use nature serves as a means — as it does for Emerson in *Nature*.[8] "To what end is nature?" Emerson asks at the beginning of his treatise, and in the section entitled "Idealism"[9] he says that it conspires to the end of disciplining us — making us, in our manipulation of nature in our daily lives, differentiate among phenomena and so perceive ideal noumena. Natural facts are symbols of spiritual facts.[10] "Nature is mediate," Emerson asserts. "It is made to serve. It receives the dominion of man as meekly as the ass on which the Saviour rode."[11]

Yet this kind of idealistic interpretation is only one side of the coin for Thoreau. Indeed, if such interpretation means that nature would be *but* a meek ass to be ridden by man to a realm elsewhere of Ideal Forms, then he would draw back. He does not wish to lose touch with the sensate world, of value in itself to him. Just two months after he speaks of nature as being able to serve as symbol of his thought, he suggests that so doing is highly inappropriate, for nature is not identical to man, however related, but a retreat from him (X, 445). Elsewhere he says he cannot value any view of the universe in which man enters largely (IX, 382), and he refers, in another instance, to the solitude he requires in nature, a nature which is "grander" than man. In expanding upon his requirement, he shows that nature here has no ulterior meaning for him. It is something to enjoy for its own sake, something in which to saturate all his senses (XII, 438–440).

Even in Thoreau's much-quoted statement — "man is all in all, Nature nothing, but as she draws him out and reflects him" (XV, 121) — Thoreau is really emphasizing in the context of the passage not so much man per se but the life that man is able to have in nature. Thoreau affirms that "life is everything" and that for him it means to walk much in fields and woods. He then makes reference to his own life there, which is a time of sensuous experiences — seeing a yellow butterfly zigzagging by a road, smelling the medicinal scent of decaying leaves after a rain. In the same volume of the *Journal*, he says that it is nature's society for which he lives. He has not, he tells us, convicted nature of folly, thus again pointing out its distinct identity and its superiority to man (XV, 210). It is partly because of these beliefs that his political essays, which castigate the ills of human society, tend to close with an optimistic note. For example, at the end of "Slavery in Massachusetts," he describes scenting a freshly-opened water lily, which had burst up "pure and fair to the eye" (IV, 407). He then does not despair so soon of the ills of the world, he says. The flower suggests an older law than that followed by man. Its fragrance suggests that man's actions will one day smell as sweet and that man must have some kindred virtue to be able to sense such beauty now.

Thoreau perhaps sees no reason for adopting a consistent view concerning man's prominence in nature. Just as he says at one place that "each gnat is made to vibrate its wings for man's fruition" (XVIII, 148), he can say in the same year (1859) that a grosbeak sings with no regard to man. Often his ideas are found to be consistent with one another if selected from a single period of his life, but he never attempts to unify his thought. Thoreau, we find, is not going to let a foolish consistency be the hobgoblin of *his* mind.[12] Why should not he have new thoughts for each new day? "A man's life should be as fresh as a river," he tells us; "it should be the same channel, but a new water every instant" (VII, 347).

What this study has attempted to show is that one consistency in Thoreau's life, one channel through which his life flows, is the sensuous approach he ever takes to the natural world. Speculating on man's place there may be important to him but so is living in nature. After associating with man, he wishes "again to participate in the serenity of nature, to share the happiness of the river and the woods" (XV, 205) with which he feels a close kinship. He writes in *Walden*:

After a still winter night I awoke with the impression that some question had been put to me, which I had been endeavoring in vain to answer in my sleep, as what — how — when — where? But there was dawning Nature, in whom all creatures live, looking in at my broad windows with serene and satisfied face, and no question on *her* lips. I awoke to an answered question, to Nature and daylight. The snow lying deep on the earth dotted with young pines, and the very slope of the hill on which my house is placed, seemed to say, Forward! Nature puts no questions and answers none which we mortals ask. (II, 312)

Thoreau awakes to an "answered question," recalling for us Emerson's poem, "The Sphinx," in which the beast calls man, because of man's continually inquiring spirit, the "*un*answered question"[13] [my italics]. This man cannot see kinship in the world — the kind Thoreau has been talking about — and so is being vanquished by distracting variety. Thoreau may well have had this poem in mind in writing this passage, for he refers to the legendary Sphinx, we remember, in the conclusion to *Walden*, and he also had written an eight-page exegesis of the poem in his *Journal* (VII, 229–237). Emerson himself makes a statement in *Nature* which has been used as a commentary on the poem and which can be turned to account here: "Every man's condition is a solution in hieroglyphic to those inquiries he would put."[14] The condition expressed in the quotation from *Walden*, we see, is one of joy and satisfaction and a solution for Thoreau. He is awake to the dawning day, and there is still more day to dawn. Nature poses no riddle; no quandary prevails.

A morning life, a time when one is fully awake *is* the "answered question." It is a time when one's senses are reinvigorated (II, 99). It is a time when all memorable events transpire. Living in nature, marching forward along its snow-covered slopes to the beat of his personal drummer who makes the day a perpetual morning — seeing, hearing, smelling, tasting, touching the natural grandeur that surrounds him — Thoreau can have no doubt of his kinship with that world, for the very act of sensing it links him to it. He can take satisfaction — whatever man's precise significance be in nature's scheme — that "there can be no very black melancholy to him who lives in the midst of nature and has his senses still" (II, 145).

Notes

Preface

1. *The Writings of Henry David Thoreau*, 20 vols., Walden edn. (Boston: Houghton Mifflin, 1906), II, 35. Volume and page citations in the text are to this, still the only full, edition. Volume I is *A Week on the Concord and Merrimack Rivers*; Volume II is *Walden*; Volume III is *The Maine Woods*; Volume IV is *Cape Cod and Miscellanies*; Volume V is *Excursions and Poems*; Volume VI is *Familiar Letters*; and Volumes VII through XX are *Journal I* through *Journal XIV*, respectively.

2. Thoreau's sexuality is not part of this study, as I have defined it. There has been at least one psychoanalytical dissertation done on Thoreau, part of which has been published, and reference is made to it in a note for Chapter 1. This area is itself subject for a separate book. For a brief discussion of Thoreau's psychosexual makeup, see Walter Harding's afterword to his revised edition of *The Days of Henry Thoreau* (New York: Dover, 1982).

3. A revised form of the address was published under the title "Thoreau" in the *Atlantic Monthly* for August of 1862. It is reprinted in Walter Harding, ed., *Thoreau: A Century of Criticism* (Dallas, Tex.: Southern Methodist University Press, 1954), pp. 22–40. The quotation here is from p. 33.

4. Alcott's words are reprinted in Harding, ed., *Thoreau: A Century of Criticism*, pp. 54–58. The quotation here is from p. 56.

5. William Ellery Channing, *Thoreau: The Poet-Naturalist* (Boston: Roberts Brothers, 1873), pp. 100–101.

6. Walter Harding, "Thoreau, Sensuous Transcendentalist," *Thoreau Journal Quarterly*, VI (1974), 4. This impression is hard to dispel. When I first had done some preliminary work on Thoreau's sensuousness and submitted, at Professor Harding's suggestion, a paper to a Canadian university quarterly, it was returned with the comment that the article assumed a "now discredited view of Thoreau."

7. Geoffrey H. Hartman, *Wordsworth's Poetry, 1787–1814* (New Haven: Yale University Press, 1964), p. xi.

8. The *Journal* too, although a record of events, is "above all . . . a work of art," as Walter Harding has stated in his foreword to *The Journal of Henry D. Thoreau*, ed. Bradford Torrey and Francis H. Allen, 14 vols. in 2 (New York: Dover, 1962), p. vii. While Thoreau may have started his journals as "exercises," over the years he came to polish what he wanted to say before making an entry: there are many preliminary drafts in existence. Therefore the *Journal* can be considered here in similar manner as are the books and essays.

9. Walter Harding, *A Thoreau Handbook* (New York: New York University Press, 1959), p. 132.

10. E. B. White, *One Man's Meat* (New York: Harper and Row, 1966), p. 118.

11. Walter Harding, *The Days of Henry Thoreau* (New York: Alfred A. Knopf, 1965), p. 296.

1 Up to One's Chin

1. The cathedral-forest image is certainly not unique to Thoreau (William Cullen Bryant and James Fenimore Cooper have used it before him), but his use of it is distinctive to him in his emphatic association of sensuous impressions with it.

2. *Consciousness in Concord: The Text of Thoreau's Hitherto "Lost Journal" (1840–41)*, ed. Perry Miller (Boston: Houghton Mifflin, 1958), p. 187. Page references to this work will be cited in the text as *LJ* followed by page number.

3. For a psychoanalytical discussion of this question, see Raymond D. Gozzi, "'Mother-Nature,'" in Walter Harding, ed., *Henry David Thoreau: A Profile* (New York: Hill and Wang, 1971), pp. 172–187. This article is a chapter from Gozzi's doctoral dissertation, "Tropes and Figures: A Psychological Study of David Henry Thoreau" (New York University, 1957). Many of the ideas in it are available through Carl Bode's essay, "The Half-Hidden Thoreau," in John Hicks, ed., *Thoreau in Our Season* (Amherst, Mass.: University of Massachusetts Press, 1966), pp. 104–116.

4. The conscious versus the unconscious approach to nature is a frequent concern of Thoreau; for example, with regard to his views on wildness (see Chapter 3) and on mysticism (see Chapter 7).

5. Thoreau's special use of the terms "washing" and "mizzling" will be discussed in Chapter 5.

6. See Morton L. Ross's discussion on kinesthesia in "*Moby-Dick* as an Education," *Studies in the Novel*, VI (1974), 67.

7. This notion, as it relates to the changing prevalence of visionary experiences in his life, will be discussed further in Chapter 7.

2 A Body All Sentient

1. There is a suggestion here too of hearing celestial sounds. This notion will be discussed in Chapter 7.

2. A discussion of Gilpin's ideas on the Picturesque, as given in such works as his *Remarks on Forest Scenery* (originally published in 1791), can be found in Carl Paul Barbier, *William Gilpin: His Drawings, Teaching, and Theory of the Picturesque* (Oxford: Clarendon Press, 1963), pp. 98–147. Barbier's book contains reproductions of many of Gilpin's paintings which well illustrate the artist's ideas.

3. How much Thoreau departs from the proponents of Picturesque beauty can be seen with further reference to Austen's novel. In Jane Austen's *Sense and Sensibility* (London: J.M. Dent, 1963), Marianne Dashwood rhapsodizes about anything picturesque, and she, we are told, would have "every book that tells her how to admire an old twisted tree" (p. 77). Edward Farrars, representing the other camp, counters by stating his dislike of crooked, blasted trees. He admires them much more "if they are tall, straight and flourishing" (p. 81). Thoreau would agree with Austen's Farrars, for he is more remembered for eulogizing arrowy pines than shrub oaks, and, although he does both, his response in each case is always determined by his unique sensuous concerns (see Chapters 8 and 6). We can note also his propensity for carrying a cane on his daily walks — not a twisted, picturesque one but a plain one whose very straightness makes it usable as a measuring rod too (see again Chapter 6).

4. Emerson previously wrote of this kind of experiment in the "Idealism" section of his essay on *Nature*, 1836. See *The Complete Works of Ralph Waldo Emerson*, 12 vols., Centenary edn. (Boston: Houghton Mifflin, 1903), Vol. I, p. 4.

3 A Horse to Himself

1. The position also parallels his views about seeing wildness in nature, to be discussed later in this chapter.

2. Inconsistencies did not overly concern Thoreau, this man who was adverse to metaphysical inquiry. A further comment on his inconsistencies appears in Chapter 8.

3. According to the *Lost Journal*, p. 164, the seasonal states of health are happiness (summer), contentment (autumn), repose (winter), and thrill (spring).

4. See Chapter 59, "Brit," of Herman Melville's *Moby-Dick*, 1851.

5. Thoreau's view here is not unrelated to the thinking of other Transcendentalists, since they held that the "cognitive act was not a knowing of things, but a having, an inner possession of them." See Sherman Paul, *The Shores of America: Thoreau's Inward Exploration* (Urbana, Ill.: University of Illinois Press, 1958), p. 7.

6. It is this kind of "wisdom" about which Thoreau's statement most fittingly applies when he says that the best "thought" is without morality (VII, 265). For a further discussion of Thoreau's views on morality and nature, see Chapter 7.

7. *The Correspondence of Henry David Thoreau*, ed. Walter Harding and Carl Bode (New York: New York University Press, 1958), p. 222. This work will be cited in the text as *Correspondence*, or as *C* followed by a page reference.

8. E. J. Rose, "The Wit and Wisdom of Thoreau's 'Higher Laws,'" *Queen's Quarterly*, LXIX (1963), 557.

9. There is also evidence to suggest that Thoreau's imagery in describing Katahdin was not even completely original but was taken, in part, from an account by one of his favorite explorers, Alexander Henry. See my article, "Alexander Henry and Thoreau's Climb of Mount Katahdin," *Thoreau Society Bulletin*, 123 (1973), 5–6.

10. See Chapter 7.

4 A Taste of Huckleberries

1. Houses weathered and unpainted blend with their settings: Thoreau's thinking here is again aligned with that of the Picturesque artists, referred to in Chapter 2. Yet the naturalness he emphasizes has its own sensuousness basis, as the next few pages in the text make clear.

2 See Theodore M. Brown, "Thoreau's Prophetic Architectural Program," *New England Quarterly*, XXXVIII (1965), 3–4.

3. William J. Griffin, in "Thoreau's Reactions to Horatio Greenough," *New England Quarterly*, XXX (1957), 508–512, argues that Thoreau's initial misunderstanding here was cleared up but that he did not change the reference in *Walden* since it suited his rhetorical purpose.

4 Daniel Defoe, *Robinson Crusoe* (Garden City, N.Y.: Doubleday Dolphin, 1945), p. 66.

5. *The Poetry of Robert Frost*, ed. Edward Connery Lathem (New York: Holt, Rinehart and Winston, 1969), pp. 101–102.

6. *Poetry of Robert Frost*, pp. 275–277.

7. *Poetry of Robert Frost*, pp. 68–69.

8. Leo Stoller comments on Thoreau's discussion of the fish trap in his *After Walden: Thoreau's Changing Views on Economic Man* (Stanford, Calif.: Stanford University Press, 1957), p. 121. While I am concerned in this chapter solely with sensuousness in Thoreau's economics, I wish to express a general indebtedness to this book.

5 Sauce to This World's Dish

1. *Complete Works of Ralph Waldo Emerson*, I, 84.
2. A Thoreauvian reflection, on the other hand, may have its *origin* in a down-to-earth image: a lilac blooming beside a decaying house speaks of the permanence of nature and the mutability of man's works.
3. *The Works of George Herbert*, ed. F. E. Hutchinson (Oxford: Clarendon Press, 1941), "Love (III)," pp. 188–189; "The Altar," p. 26; "Easter-wings," p. 43; and "The Pulley," pp. 159–160.
4. *The Poems of John Donne*, ed. Herbert J. C. Grierson, 2 vols. (London: Oxford University Press, 1912), Vol. I, "XIV" from "Holy Sonnets," p. 328; and "The good-morrow," pp. 7–8.
5. Note that Thoreau, in an early essay, "Carlyle and His Works," 1847, speaks favorably of the British writer's extravagant style.
6. The expression is Samuel Johnson's, and it appears in *Rasselas*, 1759, (Chapter X), where the author is considering the merits of the Particular versus the General in poetry, a concern of eighteenth-century writers.
7. Raymond Adams treats of this aspect of Thoreau's style in his article, "Thoreau's Mock-Heroics and the American Natural History Writers," in Wendell Glick, ed., *The Recognition of Henry David Thoreau: Selected Criticism Since 1848* (Ann Arbor, Mich.: University of Michigan Press, 1969), pp. 301–315.

6 An Appointment with a Beech Tree

1. It may be that the last word on the sensibility of plants is still to be given. Charles Darwin already in the middle of the nineteenth century had his son play a bassoon close to the leaves of a plant, but with indifferent results. He thought the leaves might vibrate to the strain. Now with sophisticated recording devices, present-day scientists are testing plant responses to various phenomena. See Peter Tompkins and Christopher Bird, "Love Among the Cabbages," *Harper's Magazine*, CCXLV (1972), 90–96.
2. Edward S. Deevey, Jr., "A Re-examination of Thoreau's *Walden*," *Quarterly Review of Biology*, XVII (1942), 1, 8.
3. Norman Foerster, *Nature in American Literature* (New York: Russell and Russell, 1950), p. 90; and Henry David Thoreau, *Thoreau's World: Miniatures from His Journal*, ed. Charles R. Anderson (Englewood Cliffs, N.J.: Prentice-Hall, 1971), p. 5.
4. See Walter Harding, *A Thoreau Handbook* (New York: New York University Press, 1959), p. 140. See also Lawrence Willson, "Thoreau and New England's

Weather," *Weatherwise*, XII (1959), 91–94, 118–124; and Ludlow Griscom, *Birds of Concord* (Cambridge, Mass.: Harvard University Press, 1949).

5. Henry David Thoreau, *Thoreau on Birds*, ed. Helen Cruickshank (New York: McGraw-Hill, 1964).

6. See Deevey, p. 8; and Philip and Kathryn Whitford, "Thoreau: Pioneer Ecologist and Conservationist," in Walter Harding, ed., *Thoreau: A Century of Criticism* (Dallas, Tex.: Southern Methodist University Press, 1954), p. 192.

7. Aldo Leopold and Sara Elizabeth Jones, "A Phenological Record for Sauk and Dane Counties, Wisconsin," *Ecological Monographs*, XVII (1947), 83.

8. Jonathan Swift, *Gulliver's Travels*, ed. Louis A. Landa (Boston: Houghton Mifflin, 1960), p. 84.

9. Walt Whitman, *Complete Poetry and Collected Prose,* ed. Justin Kaplan (New York: Library of America, 1982), pp. 409–410.

7 Hearing Beyond the Range of Sound

1. John Burroughs, "A Critical Glance into Thoreau," *Atlantic Monthly*, CXXIII (1919), 778.

2. The expression is Emerson's, from his "Introduction" to his essay on *Nature*, 1836. See *Complete Works of Ralph Waldo Emerson*, I, 3.

3. John Macy, *The Spirit of American Literature* (New York: Boni and Liveright, 1913), pp. 185–186.

4. See James Russell Lowell, "Thoreau," in Walter Harding, ed., *Thoreau: A Century of Criticism* (Dallas, Tex.: Southern Methodist University Press, 1954), p. 47.

5. Cf. Newton's picturing himself as a child on a beach with the ocean of truth undiscovered before him, referred to in the previous chapter.

6. *The Poetical Works of William Wordsworth*, ed. E. de Selincourt and Helen Darbishire, 5 vols. (Oxford: Clarendon Press, 1940–1949), Vol. V, p. 145, Bk. IV, ll. 1137–1144.

7. M. H. Abrams, *Natural Supernaturalism* (New York: W. W. Norton, 1971), p. 388.

8. *Poetical Works of William Wordsworth*, IV, 285, ll. 202–203.

9. Geoffrey H. Hartman, *Wordsworth's Poetry, 1787–1814* (New Haven: Yale University Press, 1964), p. x. See also Hartman, *The Unmediated Vision* (New Haven: Yale University Press, 1954), p. 156.

10. William Wordsworth, *The Prelude*, ed. Ernest de Selincourt (Oxford: Clarendon Press, 1926), p. 205, Bk. VI, ll. 600–602.

11. *Poetical Works of William Wordsworth*, II, 260, ll. 27, 30.

12. *Poetical Works of William Wordsworth*, V, 145, Bk. IV, ll. 1146–1147.

13. *The Complete Poetical Works of Samuel Taylor Coleridge,* ed. Ernest Hartley Coleridge, 2 vols. (Oxford: Clarendon Press, 1957), Vol. I, p. 180, l. 39.

14. *Poetical Works of William Wordsworth*, IV, 284, ll. 163–167.

15. See Hartman, *The Unmediated Vision*, p. 30.

16. See Chapter 23, "The Lee Shore," of Herman Melville's *Moby Dick*, 1851.

17. The event for him is much like what is called a *satori* in Zen Buddhism, which D. T. Suzuki describes as a realization of truth where there is yet no intellectualization. See his *Zen Buddhism: Selected Writings of D. T. Suzuki*, ed. William Barrett (Garden City, N.Y.: Doubleday Anchor, 1956), pp. 247, 184. Note, however, that Thoreau never read anything on Zen Buddhism, books on it not being available in his time.

18. A second term from Zen—*sunyata*—seems applicable here. It refers to an identity of man and nature, "but the identity does not imply the annihilation of one at the cost of the other. . . . Nature as a world of manyness is not ignored and Man as a subject facing the many remains conscious of himself." See Suzuki, p. 241.

19. Walter Harding, ed., *Thoreau, Man of Concord* (New York: Holt, Rinehart and Winston, 1960), p. 114.

20. Evelyn Underhill's book, *Mysticism* (New York: Noonday Press, 1955), is a standard work on the subject of mysticism and provides the necessary take-off point for a discussion of Thoreau's mystical feeling. Another book—R. C. Zaehner's *Mysticism Sacred and Profane* (Oxford: Clarendon Press, 1957)—also treats of the subject, particularly nature mysticism. I am not sure, however, that a book like Zaehner's, a book whose ultimate purpose is to denigrate such mysticism (the author relates it to lunacy) in order to glorify the mysticism of Christianity, and especially Roman Catholicism, is one to provide much light on those New England Transcendentalists who claimed to have, sacredly or not, a hot line to God. There is a basic lack of sympathy. In the so-called natural mystical experience, Zaehner writes, "the personality seems dissipated into the natural world" (p. 22) so that the nature mystic "is all too prone to identify Nature and God" (p. 34). Nature mysticism, then, becomes a kind of original sin where God the Creator is rejected in favor of what He has created. True mysticism, on the other hand, is defined in such a way to exclude the experiences of a Wordsworth or Thoreau. In it, the person is "wholly absorbed into the Deity Who is felt . . . as being something totally distinct" (p. 22). The experience really has nothing to do with visions or auditions—the person's body has simply "become a 'temple of the Holy Ghost'" (p. 31). The value of Zaehner's analysis, and why it is cited here, is to show that Thoreau's "mysticism," to be considered at all, must be treated on its own terms. The succeeding pages of this chapter do so, although there will still be the occasional contextual reference.

21. *The Song of God: Bhagavad-Gita*, trans. by Swami Prabhavananda and Christopher Isherwood (New York: Mentor, 1951).

22. They held that it could not be willed to come or prepared for to ensure its coming, but to avoid the passivity that could be one consequence of the doctrine, they also argued that there were certain deliberate preparations that one could undertake which would make the reception of grace more likely.

23. Note that Thoreau owned an aeolian harp.

24. *The Poetical Works of Shelley*, ed. Newell F. Ford (Boston: Houghton Mifflin, 1975), pp. 377–379.

25. *Complete Poetical Works of Samuel Taylor Coleridge*, I, 100–102.

26. See M. L. Abrams, "The Correspondent Breeze: A Romantic Metaphor," *Kenyon Review*, XIX (1957), 121–122.

27. *The Works of Henry Vaughan*, ed. L. C. Martin (Oxford: Clarendon Press, 1957), pp. 419–420.

28. Wordsworth in fact says, "Our birth is but a sleep and a forgetting." See *Poetical Works of William Wordsworth*, IV, 280, l. 58.

29. *Collected Poems of Henry Thoreau*, ed. Carl Bode (Baltimore: Johns Hopkins Press, 1964), p. 225.

30. *Poetry of Robert Frost*, pp. 121–122.

31. When a teacher, Thoreau gave the following evidence for the existence of God: he asked his pupils that if they should see the parts of a watch lying about in a shop one day and then on another day see the parts all fitted together and working in unison, would they not think that somebody with power and design had been there. Thus the earth, he told them, functions with a power overlooking all.

32. See *The Variorum Walden*, ed. Walter Harding (New York: Twayne, 1967), p. 293, n. 20.

33. The Rev. John Sylvester Smith, in "The Philosophical Naturism of Henry David Thoreau" (Drew University, Ph.D., 1948), makes this point. It is cited in Walter Harding, *A Thoreau Handbook* (New York: New York University Press, 1959), p. 142.

34. Thoreau when dying was asked if he had made his peace with God. His reply was that they had never quarreled.

35. The quotation is a paraphrase of lines 248–250 of Wordsworth's "Peter Bell": "A primrose by a river's brim / A yellow primrose was to him / And it was nothing more." The poet is making a disparaging reference to his title character. See *Poetical Works of William Wordsworth*, II, 341.

36. Walter Harding, *The Days of Henry Thoreau* (New York: Alfred A. Knopf, 1965), p. 465.

8 The Answered Question

1. Norman Foerster, *Nature in American Literature* (New York: Russell and Russell, 1950), p. 108.

2. Alan Devoe, *This Fascinating Animal World* (New York: McGraw-Hill, 1951), p. 122.

3. A. Bronson Alcott, "Thoreau," in Walter Harding, ed., *Thoreau: A Century of Criticism* (Dallas, Tex.: Southern Methodist University Press, 1954), p. 55.

4. Whitman, *Complete Poetry and Collected Prose*, p. 309, l. 33.

5. Whitman, *Complete Poetry and Collected Prose*, p. 309, l. 25.

6. *Poetical Works of William Wordsworth*, II, 214.

7. In myth, the Sphinx posed a riddle to all she met, devouring those who could not solve it. When Oedipus gave the correct answer—"Man"—she killed herself.

8. *Complete Works of Ralph Waldo Emerson*, I, 4.

9. *Complete Works of Ralph Waldo Emerson*, I, 47.

10. *Complete Works of Ralph Waldo Emerson*, I, 25.

11. *Complete Works of Ralph Waldo Emerson*, I, 40.

12. Emerson spoke of such consistencies as the product of little minds in "Self-Reliance," 1841. *Complete Works of Ralph Waldo Emerson*, II, p. 57.

13. *Complete Works of Ralph Waldo Emerson*, IX, 20–25. The quotation here is from p. 24, l. 113.

14. *Complete Works of Ralph Waldo Emerson*, IX, 412.